Organizational Performance in a Nutshell

Also by Daniel M. Wentland

Strategic Training:
Putting Employees First
ISBN-13: 978-0874259339

Organizational Performance in a Nutshell

by
Daniel M. Wentland

INFORMATION AGE PUBLISHING, INC.
Charlotte, NC • www.infoagepub.com

Library of Congress Cataloging-in-Publication Data

Wentland, Daniel M.
  Organizational performance in a nutshell / by Daniel M. Wentland.
      p. cm.
  Includes bibliographical references.
  ISBN 978-1-60752-079-5 (pbk.) – ISBN 978-1-60752-080-1 (hardcover)
1. Organizational effectiveness. 2. Industrial management. I. Title.
  HD58.9.W467 2009
  658.4'01–dc22

                                                            2009002233

Contents

Acknowledgments

First, I would like to express my appreciation to George Johnson and the staff at Information Age Publishing, who decided to publish this book. It's always difficult for a new author to get established and I am thankful for IAP's support.

Along with the publishing staff, the other most important people to thank are the readers who have decided to spend their hard-earned money on this book. I look forward to sharing many other writing projects with you.

Next, a special note of thanks to Stephen Bernhut, Susan P. Lee, and Karen Halbersleben for supporting this project.

On a personal note, I would like to recognize Suzanne and Rory Roark and Linda Watts, alias the Queen Bee, for their friendship. My wife, Kathy, always the light of my life and Samantha and Josh who are two interesting characters. The girls, Bailey and Shelby. Finally the rooties, Dakota and Scarlett, who make each day an adventure.

Introduction

How can some of the largest global organizations such as GM, Ford, Chrysler, Home Depot, Sears, Kmart, Airbus, Citigroup, Gateway, and Dell perform so poorly after being such colossal leaders in their industry?

To grapple with organizational sustainability questions, like the one above, will require a major paradigm shift in some of the most commonly held managerial and leadership beliefs. However "thinking outside the box" as the expression goes merely represents one of the challenges that must be overcome to fully understand organizational survivability.

At the most basic level, we must never forget that organizational success is first and foremost all about the people who work in the organization. How the managers and non-managerial employees relate to one another impacts the morale of the workforce and the effort that each employee is willing to exert. At a deeper level, a non-combative, productive managerial-employee relationship hinges upon the notion of an individual's self-concept. Our self-concept is how we perceive our self and it's that perception that influences our behavior with other individuals and the world at large. We can think of our self-concept as our rule-set or as Lincoln Child (2006) wrote in his fictional work titled *Death Match*, "Everyone lives by a set of internal rules, whether they know it or not. You understand enough of a person's rules, you can understand, predict their behavior" (p. 143). Examining our self-concept and having the ability to move beyond our self sets the stage for understanding how to achieve the maximum effort from each employee, not the minimum.

Organizational Performance in a Nutshell, pages ix–x
Copyright © 2009 by Information Age Publishing

In all cultures, human beings have been driven by the same imperatives: to be intelligent, responsible, reasonable, living and, if necessary, to change. The very nature of humanity, therefore, demands that we transcend ourselves and our current perceptions, and this principle indicates the presence of what has been called the divine in the very nature of serious human inquiry. (Armstrong, 1993, p. 385)

Or as stated by Albert Einstein, "The true value of a human being is determined primarily by the measure and the sense in which he has attained to liberation from the self" (1995, pp. 7–8).

Liberation from the self begins our journey towards discovering the five definitive keys to organizational success. With an understanding of the five keys the seemingly unsolvable fluctuations in the performance of various organizations will once and for all be summarized in a straight forward, comprehensive framework. Put simply, the ultimate objective of this book is to provide you, the reader, with the definitive explanation of why an organization can fall prey to obsolescence, wither, and eventually become extinct destined to become a faded memory in a business game version of trivial pursuit?

In other words, organizational performance in a nutshell will be revealed.

References

Armstrong, K. (1993). *A history of God.* New York: Ballantine Books.

Child, L. (2006). *Death match.* New York: Anchor Books.

Einstein, A. (1995). *The world as I see it.* New York: Citadel Press.

PART 1

The Starting Point

1

A Glimpse into Organizational Performance

An organization survives "by offering the public something that is worth the surrender of money."

—John Kenneth Galbraith (1983, p. 63)

One day while enjoying a delicious Chick-fil-A chicken sandwich I happened to look at a sign posted on one of the walls in the restaurant. The sign was titled "Never on Sundays" and the words written on the sign describe what it means to be a great place to work.

People always ask us, "Why are you closed on Sunday?" We respect the hard work of our employees. As a result, we believe in giving them the day off to worship, if they choose, or spend time with family and friends

Chick-fil-A moved beyond talking about putting their employees first by establishing policies and practices that clearly demonstrated the company's concern for its employees. To improve productivity and the organizational

Organizational Performance in a Nutshell, pages 3–5

3

commitment of the employees it's the actions of management that count, not their words.

The difference between actions and words was highlighted in a recent *Wall Street Journal* article (Kent, 2005). In that article it was reported that most organizations do not practice what they preach; despite the claims of a majority of executives that their organizations treat employees with respect and offer fair pay for the tasks performed. The disconnection between what organizational leaders claim they do and what they actually do is partly attributable to a marketing philosophy that began to dominate management theory after the production, product, and selling concepts faded in popularity. At the center of this philosophy is the notion that the customer should be the focus of all organizational activities and planning.

Although the emphasis upon the customer appears to be a logical starting point for building organizational success, it is actually quite misleading: Simply put, many organizations do not know who their customers are! For example, who is the customer at a college or university? High school graduates? Adults returning to college? Graduate students? Foreign students? Or individuals seeking a vocational trade? And what is the socio-economic and demographic data associated with these classifications of students? Who is the customer for a retailer like Wal-Mart? Is it the person who drives a Mercedes to Wal-Mart in order to purchase everyday items at lower prices? Or is it the individual who uses public transportation to arrive at the store? A customer who cannot be specifically identified in every detail is an illusion, and illusions serve as a poor basis for building successful strategy.

And even if the "customer" was completely identified, should he or she be placed at the center of every organizational activity? Doing so, I believe, pushes aside the true essence of the organization, minimizing its significance. The heart of an organization is its employees. The abilities, decisions, plans, training, and actions of the employees of an organization are what draw individuals to a particular college or retailer or even to purchase a product or pay for a service. The primary driving force that brings people into a concert hall is to hear enchanting music performed by trained musicians whose skills and talents are on display. Highly qualified employees produce quality products and provide quality service that satisfies consumer needs.

An organization's employees have always made the difference between a truly successful organization and a mediocre entity, but it's amazing how often managers overlook or discount this fundamental recipe for economic survival. Organizations with cultures that focus on their people and that invest in their future will, in the long run, be more competitive than cultures that view employees as mere costs to be reduced in times of trouble.

However, as important as the commitment to the employees is, that concept represents just a glimpse into organizational performance. As we venture further into the realm of organizational sustainability we will uncover the five definitive keys to organizational success. The path leading to the discovery of those keys will lead us through many topics but when we come to the end of our journey the secrets behind why great organizations are great and mediocre organizations are just that will be exposed. In sum, organizational performance in a nutshell will be revealed once and for all.

The Critical Points in the Chapter that Lead to the Discovery of the Five Definitive Keys to Organizational Success and Sustainability

Critical Point 1

To maximize output an organization needs to put employees first. Many organizations claim to put their employees first—few do.

Critical Point 2

As important as the commitment to the employees is, that concept represents just a glimpse into organizational performance. Ultimately, organizational performance depends upon understanding the five definitive keys to organizational success and sustainability.

References

Galbraith, J. K. (1983). *The anatomy of power.* Boston, MA: Houghton Mifflin.

Kent, S. (September 6, 2005). Happy workers are the best workers. *Wall Street Journal*, p. A20.

Wentland, D. M. (2007). *Strategic training: Putting employees first.* Amherst, MA: HRD Press, pp. vii, viii.

2

Changing the Management–Employee Paradigm

The best piece of business is one in which everyone walks away a winner.
—Dean Koontz (2006, pp. 298–299)

How can one or a few organizations thrive while others in the same industry struggle for survival? How can organizational performance be outstanding one year and average or worse the following year? Why does a company with a productive workforce fail in the marketplace? Why are so many individuals disappointed with their work environment? What drives productivity and value creation? What denotes a great place to work from a miserable one? How can some of the largest global organizations fail to meet performance standards and financial objectives? What determines organizational performance?

When analyzing organizational phenomena one needs to have a clear understanding of what constitutes an organization. In his book, John Sey-

Organizational Performance in a Nutshell, pages 7–10
Copyright © 2009 by Information Age Publishing
All rights of reproduction in any form reserved.

farth (1999) cites Pasmore's definition of an organization. "Organizations are composed of people who use tools, techniques, and knowledge to produce goods or services that are valued by members or customers." Pasmore (1988) further stated that "when members of an organization are aware of the demands of the external environment and are able to apply their skills to meet those demands, the organization is likely to be effective, but when something interferes with their ability to respond to environmental demands, the organization is less productive." With Pasmore's (1988) definition serving as our characterization of an organization we can extract three elements common to all organizations. People or the members of an organization are the first and most important element. Flowing from the people or members of an organization are the other two elements: purpose and (or) goals as well as the structure (meaning the hierarchy.) As I stated in my first book, *Strategic Training: Putting Employees First* (Wentland, 2007), without people the other two elements of an organization would cease to exist since those elements are the product of the members. Thus the knowledge, skills, and abilities of the managerial and non-managerial members are the most important internal part of an organization.

How managers have traditionally utilized their organizational authority is one of the fundamental issues being challenged in this book for I'm proposing that the time has arrived for a paradigm shift in the relationship between management and the non-managerial members (employees). Management must come to the realization that organizational performance is enhanced when they view employees as partners not subordinates; in other words management must put the employees first—and mean it. The managerial philosophy of putting the employees first and reinforcing that philosophy through the policies and practices established by management is one of the features that distinguish this book from many other leadership and management information sources. Management retains the final decision-making authority but the focus should be upon how an organizational decision impacts the employees for that in turn will influence how the employees perform their job and ultimately how they interact with the customer.

As for the employees they must continually strive for excellence in every task they perform as management loosens the grip of power and accepts the employees as equal partners. As stated by Peters and Waterman, Jr. (2004) in their seminal work, *In Search of Excellence,* "productivity and the economic rewards that go with it are achieved through the people of an organization." The importance of changing the management–employee paradigm is an organizational philosophy that I will continually stress.

Changing the Management–Employee Relationship Paradigm

Management must view the employees as partners not subordinates and put the employees ahead of any other factor that impacts the organization	**+**	Employees must continually strive for excellence in every task they perform as management loosens the grip of power and adopts a managerial attitude that views employees as partners not subordinates	**=**	Employees exert a maximum effort because the employees understand that the organization is truly concerned about them. Productivity and customer satisfaction should increase

How does your organization treat you? Do you feel "truly" appreciated at work? Does your organization act as if you are its most important asset or just another cost? How does the attitude of your organization impact the effort you are willing to put forth?

After studying management, leadership, organizational behavior, marketing, and economics since the 1980s and having worked as a national new accounts and customer service manager for Citigroup this author has come to the conclusion that managers who establish policies and practices that clearly demonstrate a true concern for the employees will create a work environment where the employees are more likely to put forth the maximum effort to take care of the customer; not the minimum.

Bringing about a paradigm shift in the management-employee relationship will not be easy for many organizations claim to put their employees first, but few do.

So what's the next step? Understanding organizational performance begins with understanding ourselves and the right kind of leader that is required to sustain organizational effectiveness and efficiency. Then we'll examine group and organizational dynamics as well as the external forces that impact an organization.

The bottom line is that when our journey is finished the critical variables that shape organizational performance will no longer be a mystery; for just like Sherlock Holmes is able to uncover and decipher the vital clues that unravel a perplexing case so will we succeed in our search for the keys that unlock the secrets behind organizational success and sustainability.

The Critical Points in the Chapter that Lead to the Discovery of the Five Definitive Keys to Organizational Success and Sustainability

Critical Point 1

The management–employee relationship paradigm needs to become more of a partnership rather than being viewed as an arrangement in which one group is subordinate to the other.

Critical Point 2

Organizations that adopt the new management–employee relationship and demonstrate a clear concern for their employees will create a workplace in which employees are more likely to put forth a maximum effort; not a minimum.

Critical Point 3

Understanding organizational performance begins with understanding ourselves and the right kind of leader that is required to sustain organizational effectiveness and efficiency.

References

Koontz, D. (2006). *The husband.* New York: Bantam Books.

Pasmore, W. (1988). *Designing effective organizations: The sociotechnical systems perspective.* New York: Wiley.

Peters, T., & Waterman, R., Jr. (2004). *In search of excellence.* New York: Harper Business Essentials.

Seyfarth, J. T. (1999). *The principal: New leadership for new challenges.* Upper Saddle River, NJ: Merrill/Prentice-Hall.

Wentland, D. M. (2007). *Strategic training: Putting employees first.* Amherst, MA: HRD Press.

PART **2**

Unmasking Ourselves and Discovering
the Right Leader

3

The Voyage

The human brain is the most complicated structure in the known universe, but brains still know very little about themselves. . . . It's almost as if you need someone else to tell you who you are, or to hold up the mirror for you.

—Michael Crichton (2002, p. 95)

I hope you don't mind if a non-fiction author tries his hand at creating a brief tale about life and self-discovery for our quest to discover the five definitive keys of organizational performance must begin by looking inward and unmasking who we are and understanding how our behavior influences the workplace.

A Tale About Life and Self-Discovery

As I looked into the night sky I wanted to reach up and touch the stars. But as I raised my hands towards the heavens I knew that the sparkling objects seemingly adrift in the calm, dark waters of a faraway ocean were many light years away.

How far does the universe extend? What are its boundaries? Does the universe have any boundaries? As these questions fueled my imagination, I suddenly felt as if mankind was being drawn back to the days of Columbus, who standing upon the shores of the mighty Atlantic, dreamed of discovering a New World. A world that would forever establish the boundaries of the Earth—like a painting set within its frame.

With my thoughts still drifting among the stars, I wondered what new adventures a-wait our species; what new mysteries would mankind uncover? But most of all I was trying to visualize how our lives would change as we continue to unlock what was once unknown?

The unknown, the gray area of life, offers so many mysteries the most haunting of which is the quest to uncover the meaning of life. Does life have a purpose? Is there a natural order to the universe? Is there a universal plan? Can the answers to these questions be found in some faraway location in the universe? Do the stars that dot the heavenly landscape mark the trail to that location—like glimmering points on a celestial map or will mankind be destined to roam upon many paths that never quite lead us to the answers we so desperately seek?

As these thoughts completely engulfed my consciousness, like a thick fog rumbling across a field swallowing up everything in sight, the glowing light of the sun began to slowly appear near the horizon and soon the darkness gave way to the birth of a new day. As the soothing rays of the rising sun gently reached out and touched my face, I suddenly realized that the meaning of life is not found by searching through some remote corner of the universe but will only be revealed through an exploration of the soul. Life is about what we think, what we believe in, how we live our daily life, and most important, how we treat others.

Life is a voyage of self-discovery and the heavenly light of the stars seem to possess an almost mystical ability to inspire each of us to search deep with-in our soul and probe for the answers that explain why we are the way we are. An intensive, private inquiry that will eventually unmask our "real" identity as every layer of our "outer being" gets peeled away until our "inner being" lies totally exposed. Only after such a journey will our mind and heart be opened to the realization of how we either positively or negatively influence the environment around us.

Gaining a "true" sense of who we are can pose a significant challenge at the individual level:

There's one problem with all psychological knowledge—nobody can apply it to themselves. People can be incredibly astute about the shortcomings of their friends, spouses, children. But they have no insight into themselves at all.... When people turn their psychological insight-apparatus on themselves ... the brain hangs The thought process goes and goes, but it doesn't get anywhere. It must be something like that, because we know that people can think about themselves indefinitely. Some people think of little else. Yet people never seem to change as a result of their intensive introspection. They never understand themselves better. It's very rare to find genuine self-knowledge. It's almost as if you need someone else to tell you who you are, or to hold up the mirror for you.... You have to start seeing things as they really are, and not as you want them to be" (Crichton, 2002, pp. 77–78)

To see things as they really are requires a thorough internal analysis that can lead us to an understanding of our behavior. Behavior is based on an individual's perception of a situation, their personality, environmental factors including culture and life experiences, their attitudes and motivational influences all combined together like ingredients in a recipe being mixed together to form a particular dish. It is the differences in perception, personality, environmental factors, attitudes and motivation that makes each person unique and accounts for our individual differences and behaviors. In fact, the term, individual differences, refers to the notion that people differ in a variety of ways.

Focusing upon understanding individual behavior constitutes the first leg of the voyage towards understanding the five definitive keys of organizational success since individual behavior certainly influences group and organizational outcomes. Sometimes the behavior of an individual can have an immediate impact upon an organization such as employee theft. In other instances the ramifications upon the organization are more cumulative and long-term in nature such as a series of poor strategic management decisions leading to a perpetual state of under performance and a lack of competitiveness in the marketplace. Whether the impact is immediate or more long-term the behavior and actions of individuals set the parameters that limit what a group or organization can achieve. From a management standpoint, as stated by Stephen Robbins (2001, p. 36): "the issue revolves around knowing how people differ in abilities and using that knowledge to increase the likelihood that an employee will perform his or her job well."

Maximizing employee performance begins with an understanding of the intellectual and physical abilities of the employee and then matching those abilities to the job. When the employee ability-job match is out of equilibrium, either because the employee's abilities exceed or are not sufficient to perform the task, the performance level of the employee will be marginal at best. Marginally performing employees result in under-performing groups and unproductive, non-competitive organizations.

On the other hand, when the employee ability-job match is in equilibrium the stage is set for gains in productivity at the individual employee, group, or organizational level.

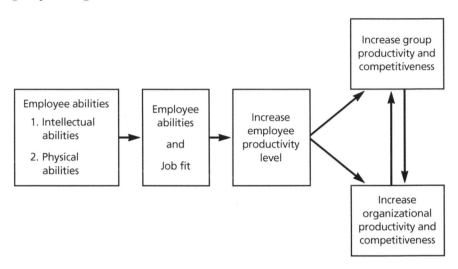

Employee productivity is a driving force that influences organizational competitiveness in the marketplace which in turn is rooted in the premise that to ultimately flush out what maximizes organizational performance requires an exploration of the self. Only through an examination of the self can we begin the process of understanding the right type of leader, meaning a leader with the right self-image and right self-concept to want to create a workplace in which the traditional management–employee relationship paradigm is cast aside in favor of the new management–employee relationship paradigm that was outlined in chapter two. Moving to the new management–employee paradigm is an essential step if an organization wants to maximize the work product of each employee.

A journey towards uncovering the self will reveal what lurks beneath the relationship between productivity and the matching of the abilities of an employee to a particular job. In fact, understanding our inner self is like the unseen portion of an iceberg that lies below the waterline and it is what lies beneath the waterline that can be extremely dangerous; the ill-fated voyage of the Titanic will always serve to remind us of that.

Individual Level Analysis Influencing Group and Organizational Outcomes

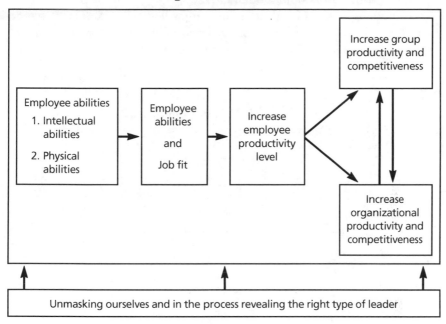

In sum, the process of unmasking ourselves begins the journey that must be followed in order to truly comprehend organizational performance and sustainability; the issue now becomes—do you want to continue this voyage? Do you want to see what is at the core of your being and more importantly—how you influence the workplace? If so, I invite you to read on.

The Critical Points in the Chapter that Lead to the Discovery of the Five Definitive Keys to Organizational Success and Sustainability

Critical Point 1

Unmasking ourselves forms the foundation upon which individual, group, and organizational performance can thrive or wither. Understanding ourselves and how we influence the workplace is the first leg of our journey towards discovering the five definitive key of organizational success.

Critical Point 2

Only through an examination of the self can we begin the process of understanding the right type of leader, meaning a leader who wants to change the traditional management–employee paradigm to the new management–employee relationship that was outlined in chapter 2.

References

Crichton, M. (2002). *Prey.* New York: Harper Collins.

Robbins, S. (2001). *Organizational behavior* (9th ed.). Upper Saddle River, NJ: Prentice Hall.

4

Perception

A man had just purchased the car of his dreams. It was a fire engine red, sleek and powerful corvette with every available option. The man had just picked up his dream car from the dealership and immediately headed to the open roads of the country where he could test and feel the power of his new racing automobile. Within a half hour the crowded streets of the city gave way to open landscape of the country. Driving with the convertible top down the man felt the sun on his face and was completely enjoying the breeze rushing through his hair as the car soared like an eagle over the road. Suddenly, as the man was approaching a sharp curve another car driven by a quite attractive woman raced around the curve swerving wildly across the lane heading directly for the man. At the last second, the female driver gained control over her vehicle and steered the car back into the proper driving lane. As the vehicles passed within inches of each other the female driver shouted the word "Pig" in an agitated tone. Immediately the driver of the corvette responded with what he felt was an appropriate hand gesture given the actions of the female driver. After issuing his hand gesture, the driver of the corvette hit the gas pedal and raced around the curve crashing into an enormous pig that was standing in the road.

—Anonymous

In this chapter we wrestle with the "reality of perception"

As we journey through the daily routine of life every minute we spend on this planet defines who we are, why we behave the way we do, and how

---

Organizational Performance in a Nutshell, pages 19–24

we react to other people. Ultimately, the behavior of any individual is a function of their perception of the environment that surrounds them, their personality, their attitudes and motivational influences. An interesting peek into the behavior of the first President of the United States was illustrated in an exhibition titled *Treasures From Mount Vernon: George Washington Revealed at The New-York Historical Society building in New York City*. While wandering around the numerous displays of documents, clothing, pictures, furniture, and a miniature model of Mount Vernon—I stumbled upon a letter written by an individual who wrote the following "I have attended many occasions at Mount Vernon and have noticed that Mr. Washington rarely speaks and when he does it is never about himself;" a revealing comment about the inner being of one person from the observations of another.

Unmasking our inner being, the self beneath the shell of our body, involves an analysis of perception, personality, attitudes and motivational influences.

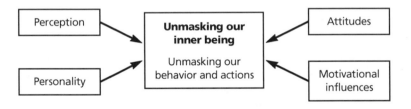

Perception is the selection and organization of environmental stimuli to provide meaningful experiences for the perceiver. Perception involves searching for, obtaining, and processing information. Perception represents the psychological process whereby people take information from the environment and make sense of their worlds.

How we perceive our environment is influenced by internal and external factors. Internal perception factors include attitudes, motives, interests, personality, learning experiences, cultural background and expectations. All of these factors are aspects of the person (or perceiver)—the individual looking at a target and attempting to interpret what he (or she) sees. External factors are characteristics that influence whether the stimuli will be noticed. For our purposes "the stimuli" can be referred to as any environmental event that may produce a response in an organism. External perception factors include characteristics in the target—what is being perceived (observed) and the situation—characteristics in the immediate environment that influence our perception.

External Perception Factors (Characteristics in the target)

Size—the larger the size, the more likely the factor will be perceived

Intensity—the more intense (bright lights, loud noises, intensity of writing), the more likely the factor will be perceived

Background (Contrast)—factors that stand out against a background or that are not what people expect are more likely to be perceived

Motion—a moving factor is more likely to be perceived

Repetition—a repeated factor is more likely to be perceived

Novelty or Familiarity—either a familiar or a novel factor in an environment attracts attention, depending on the circumstances

Proximity—objects that are close to each other will tend to be perceived together rather than separately. As a result of physical or time proximity, we often put together objects or events that are unrelated.

External Perception Factors (Characteristics of the situation)

Time—the time of day can influence what might be perceived

Work setting—a particular situation, under a particular set of circumstances, in a particular work setting might increase the chances of being noticed and influence our perception

Social setting—a particular situation, under a particular set of circumstances, in a particular social setting might increase the chances of being noticed and influence our perception.

Source: Robbins (2001).

To illustrate the importance of perception, let's consider a thought experiment that Albert Einstein utilized when developing the Theories of Special and General Relativity. The thought experiment grappled with the question of whether two individuals would see two bolts of lighting (traveling at an identical speed and distance) strike two poles at the same time if one of the individuals was in a moving train while the other was standing halfway between the two poles? Both individuals would be holding a specially designed mirror that would allow each of them to continually see the lighting as well as the two poles. Given this set-up, the experiment provided a theoretical methodology for evaluating whether two individuals witnessing the same event would see the same thing (the same reality). Using common sense, we probably would predict that the two individuals would see the lighting bolts strike the poles at the same time since each of the bolts of lighting would be traveling at the same speed and distance towards the poles. Unfortunately, that evaluation would lead us to an incorrect conclusion because the individual positioned in the moving train would first see the lighting strike the pole in the direction that the train was heading and then witness the other pole being struck. The person standing half way between the two poles would see the lighting bolts strike the poles at the same time. For us, the story illustrates the notion of perception and how two individuals observing the same situation (environment) may not see the same thing and that creates a problem when we are trying to objectively examine our inner being and the environment in which we live.

The bending and twisting of reality that perception can create stems from two sources. The first source relates to the internal and external perception factors that were previously outlined. The second source (referred to as the *self-serving bias*) focuses upon our tendency as human beings to attribute our successes to internal factors while placing the blame for failures on external factors. In other words, when we succeed at something our perception is that the success was achieved primarily because of our efforts while at the other end of the spectrum, our failures and disappointments are perceived as occurring because of outside forces not under our control. The self-serving bias allows us to mentally "pass the buck" regarding our actions and provides a convenient outlet for not taking responsibility for our decisions which when left unchecked can easily lead to a complete divorce from what had actually transpired. This separation from reality forms an effective barrier to honest and sincere self-analysis—an analysis that must occur because we need to understand who we are and how our behavior and actions influence the performance outcomes that can be achieved at the individual, group or organizational level.

The Role of Perception in Unmasking Ourselves and the Affect Upon Individual, Group, and Organizational Performance

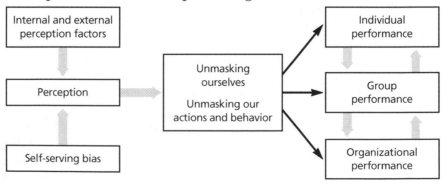

Given the illusionary barriers that can be erected as a result of an individual's perception how can the veil of misperception be pulled back so that we can objectively see who we are and how we influence the environment around us? No easy answer exists but an examination of the attribution process can provide some guidance.

> The attribution process refers to the ways in which people come to understand the causes of others' (and their own) behaviors. Attributions play an important role in the process of person perception. Attributions made about the reasons for someone's behavior may affect judgments about that individual's fundamental characteristics or traits (what he or she is "really like")....The attributions that employees and managers make concerning the causes of behavior are important in understanding behavior in organizations. For example, managers who attribute poor performance directly to their subordinates tend to behave more punitively than managers who attribute poor performance to circumstances beyond their subordinates' control. A manager who believes that an employee failed to perform a task correctly because she lacked proper training might be understanding and give the employee better instructions or training. The same manager might be quite angry if he believes that a subordinate made mistakes simply because the subordinate did not try very hard (Hellriegel, Slocum, & Woodman, 1995, pp. 90–95)

In the end, the relationship between attributions and an individual's perception of success or failure are linked to four causal factors: ability, effort, task difficulty, and luck. Causal attributions of ability and effort are internal (under the direct control of the individual) while causal attributions of task difficulty and luck are external (not under the direct control of the individual).

Internal Attributions

I succeeded (or failed) because I had the skills to do the job (or because I did not have the skills to do the job). Such statements are ability attributions.

I succeeded (or failed) because I worked hard (or because I did not work hard). Such statements are effort attributions.

External Attributions

I succeeded (or failed) because it was easy (or because it was too hard). Such statements are attributions about task difficulty.

I succeeded (or failed) because I was lucky (or unlucky). Such statements are attributions about luck or the circumstances surrounding the task.

Source: Hellriegel, Slocum, & Woodman, 1995

The four causal factors of success or failure not only play a pivotal role in analyzing and dissecting how an individual's perception of a situation might blur reality but more importantly, the four causal factors of success or failure provide an individual with a mechanism for gaining some insight into his or her behavior and actions. The more an individual understands their behavior and actions the further that individual can walk down the path that leads them towards unmasking who they really are.

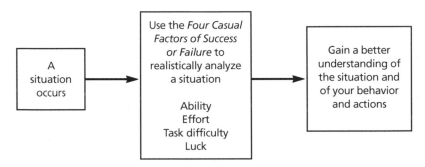

The next leg in our voyage of self-discovery will plunge us into a deeper understanding of who we really are by examining the basics of personality.

The Critical Points in the Chapter that Lead to the Discovery of the Five Definitive Keys to Organizational Success and Sustainability

Critical Point 1

Perception influences our behavior and actions and thus provides a glimpse into unmasking who we really are.

Critical Point 2

The *Four Casual Factors of Success or Failure* can be utilized to realistically analyze a situation and diagnose our behavior and actions. Ultimately, this diagnosis allows us to continue our voyage towards discovering what lies at the core of our being.

References

Hellriegel, D., Slocum J., & Woodman, R. (1995). *Organizational behavior* (7th ed.). St. Paul, MN: West Publishing Company.

Robbins, S. (2001). *Organizational behavior* (9th ed.). Upper Saddle River, NJ: Prentice Hall.

5

A Deeper Plunge Into Ourselves

The Basics of Personality

Why are people different?

Perception can cloud our judgment, skew our notion of reality and warp our understanding of who we really are. To burrow beneath the flesh and bones that form our physical image we have to take an objective look into our spirit. As the misunderstood hero in the movie *Shrek* stated to his donkey companion during their journey to rescue the princess "an ogre has many layers" and it's time for us to peel back the layers that cover up our personality—the core of our being.

Personality can be referred to as consistency in behavior and how we react to events and situations. Debate continues regarding the degree to which our personality is determined by nature (heredity and genetics) or environmental factors such as culture, family, group membership, and life experiences (nurture). In addition to these two factors, a third dimension of personality focuses upon the interplay between the situation and the individual. Although, one's personality tends to be stable and consistent—un-

Organizational Performance in a Nutshell, pages 25–31

der different situations a particular aspect of an individual's personality can dominate the behavior of a person. For example, a non-violent individual placed in a life-threatening situation will probably become quite violent in order to survive. These three dimensions of personality (heredity, nurture, and the situation) form a complex web that drives our behavior and provides important clues to examining our inner being—the true entity that exists within the walls of our flesh.

Stemming from the three dimensions of personality, like flowers blossoming on the vine, are the various theories that attempt to explain our behavior. These theories create a pool of information that increases the body of knowledge regarding personality—an intellectual expansion that ultimately moves us closer to understanding ourselves. The theories of personality can generally be divided along two broad "schools of thought"—descriptive theories of personality versus developmental theories of personality.

Personality Theories

Descriptive Theories	Developmental Theories
Type theories which classify people into a certain personality type (Type A & B personalities, Myers-Briggs Type Indicator, and Internalizers-Externalizers)	*Psychoanalytic* theories of personality development tend to portray human motivation as self-interested and uncivilized unless socially acceptable roles and outlets are provided
Trait theories which are enduring characteristics or tendencies that describe an individual's behavior (16 Primary Traits, The "Big Five" Personality Factors)	*Humanistic* theories assume that human nature is essentially positive, productive, and growth-oriented, and that people would develop in healthy ways if they knew how
	Learning theories apply basic principles of learning to the development and function of personality

Type Theories

An individual with a Type A personality tends to have the following characteristics: impatient, concerned with time and punctuality, very competitive, obsessed with numbers, measures their success in terms of money or how much of everything they acquire and strives to think or do two or more things at once. Type B individuals tend to be more relaxed, take one thing at a time, expresses their feelings, never suffer from a sense of time urgency, feel no need to display or discuss either their achievements or accomplishments unless such exposure is demanded by the situation and can relax without guilt.

The Myers–Briggs Type Indicator is loosely based on the personality theories of Carl Jung (1885–1961) and was originally published in 1943 by Katharine C. Briggs and Isabel Briggs Myers. Basically the Myers–Briggs Type Indicator is a self-assessment personality test that in the end characterizes an individual along four dimensions.

The Four Dimensions	Description of Personality Types
Problem-Solving Orientation	
Introverted	The introverted person is shy and withdrawn, likes a quiet environment for concentration, dislikes interruptions, and is content to work alone
Extroverted	The extroverted person is outgoing, often aggressive, likes variety, likes to function in a social environment, often acts quickly without thinking, and may dominate situations or people
Information Gathering Dimensions	
Sensation type	Sensing types like action and focus on getting things done, they work steadily and reach a conclusion step by step
Intuition type	Intuitive types dislike doing the same thing repeatedly, enjoy learning new skills, may leap to a conclusion quickly, and often follow their inspirations and hunches
Decision-Making Dimensions	
Thinking type	Thinking types excel at putting things in logical order, respond more to people's ideas than feelings, need to be treated fairly, and tend to be firm and tough-minded
Feeling type	Feeling types like harmony, respond to individual's values and feelings, as well as their thoughts, tend to be sympathetic, and enjoy pleasing people
Evaluating Dimensions	
Judgment type	Judgment types like to get thing finished and work best with a plan; they dislike interrupting their projects and tasks and use lists as agendas
Perception type	Perception types adapt well to changing situations and do not mind last-minute changes; they may begin many projects but experience difficulty in finishing them or may postpone unpleasant tasks

Source: Gordon (1996).

Classifying personality types according to Internalizers versus External-izers wrestles with the issue of whether or not a person believes he or she controls their own destiny. Internalizers are individuals who believe they control their own life and are primarily responsible for what occurs within their life while externalizers perceive that forces outside of their own con-trol determine their fate. Externalizers view themselves as pawns of luck, chance and the actions of others.

Trait Theories

The 16 Primary Traits model of personality classifies human behavior among 16 traits. According to this theory, an individual displays these traits in a consistent manner and therefore the traits tentatively provide an expla-nation of a person's behavior.

Sixteen Primary Traits

1. Reserved vs. Outgoing
2. Less Intelligent vs. More Intelligent
3. Affected by feelings vs. Emotionally Stable
4. Submissive vs. Dominant
5. Serious vs. Happy-go-lucky
6. Expedient vs. Conscientious
7. Timid vs. Venturesome
8. Tough-minded vs. Sensitive
9. Trusting vs. Suspicious
10. Practical vs. Imaginative
11. Forthright vs. Shrewd
12. Self-assured vs. Apprehensive
13. Conservative vs. Experimenting
14. Group-dependent vs. Self-sufficient
15. Uncontrolled vs. Controlled
16. Relaxed vs. Tense

The "Big Five" personality factors approach reduces the number of traits that are utilized to explain behavior. According to this theory, an in-dividual's personality is encapsulated along a continuum derived from five primary factors (adjustment, sociability, conscientiousness, agreeableness, and intellectual openness).

The "Big Five" Personality Factors

$\longleftarrow$ —————————————————————————————— $\longrightarrow$

Adjustment
(Stable, confident, effective)   (Nervous, self-doubting, moody)

Sociability
(Gregarious, energetic, self-dramatizing)   (Shy, unassertive, withdrawn)

Conscientiousness
(Plan, neat, dependable)   (Impulsive, careless, irresponsible)

Agreeableness
(Warm, tactful, considerate)   (Independent, cold, rude)

Intellectual Openness
(Imaginative, curious, original)   (Dull, unimaginative, literal-minded)

Source: Hellriegel, Slocum, & Woodman, 1995

Psychoanalytic Theories

Like the roots of a plant reaching deep into the soil bringing forth the nutrients required for life, the foundation for most psychoanalytic theories is grounded in the ideas of Sigmund Freud (1856–1939). According to Freud:

> The individual at birth has no personality or public "persona" yet. The infant is completely selfish and motivated by the pleasure principle, the drive to seek physical pleasure and satisfaction. This is embodied in a part of the personality known as the *id.* In the course of early childhood discipline the child develops ideas of right and wrong, permitted and forbidden behavior. The understanding that some acts are wrong comprises one's conscience, while the gradual understanding of what is good and socially rewarded becomes one's ego ideal (idealized self). Together the conscience and ego ideal make up the *superego.* The superego guides and shapes the primitive id, inducing guilt when one has behaved selfishly or badly, and permitting a sense of pride when one has behaved well. Between the selfish urges of the id and the almost unrealistic admonitions of the superego, one develops an *ego,* a self that is largely visible (in contrast with the completely unconscious id and partially unconscious superego). The ego abides by the reality principle, effecting compromise that will satisfy some of the id's demands while not violating too many of the superego's constraints. (Weber, 1991, p. 169)

Humanistic Theories

According to William James (1842–1910) an individual's personality consists of four "selves" a material self, a social self, a spiritual, and one's psychological faculties.

The Four "Selves"	Description
1. Material Self	Includes one's physical body and material possessions
2. Social Self	Consists of how one is viewed by others
3. Spiritual Self	Consists of one's spiritual thoughts and beliefs
4. Psychological faculties	Includes reasoning and feeling; and the pure ego, maintained in one's ongoing awareness or stream of consciousness

Source: Weber, 1991, p. 172

Learning Theories

Learning is defined as a relatively permanent change in human capabilities that is not a result of growth processes. These capabilities are related to specific learning outcomes (verbal information, intellectual skills, motor skills, attitudes and cognitive strategies). Several learning theories can be utilized to provide a foundation for understanding how an individual is motivated to learn and how the learning experience molds one's personality and behavior. (a) Reinforcement theory emphasizes that people are motivated to perform or avoid certain behaviors because of past outcomes that have resulted from those behaviors; (b) Social learning theory suggests that individuals first watch others who act as models and then behave according to what they have witnessed; (c) Goal setting theory implies that establishing and committing to specific and challenging goals can influence an individual's behavior; (d) Need Theories (Maslow's Hierarchy of Needs, Alderfer's ERG Theory, Herzberg's Dual-Structure Theory and David McClelland's Need Theory) assume that need deficiencies cause behavior; (e) Expectancy theory implies that an individual's behavior is a function of three factors (expectancy, instrumentality, and valence). The expectancy factor refers to an individual's belief that effort will lead to a particular performance level and that the performance level is associated with a particular outcome (instrumentality factor) and that the outcome is valued by the individual (valence factor).

What can generally be gained from the theories of personality is threefold. First, personality theory offers a framework for evaluating the extent to which a person believes that he or she is a worthwhile and deserving individual (self-esteem) and secondly, based on a person's self-esteem an individual's actions and behaviors can be better understood. Thirdly, embedded in an individual's personality is the rigidity of that person's beliefs and his or her openness to other viewpoints (dogmatism).

From an organizational perspective, personality theory can provide a glimpse into a person's beliefs about his or her capabilities to perform a task (self-efficacy), the degree to which an individual is willing to take chances and make risky decisions (risk propensity), and the extent to which an individual believes that power and status differences are appropriate within hierarchical social systems like organizations (authoritarianism).

Ultimately, the theories of personality move us a step closer towards discovering the right type of leader, meaning an individual who can easily adapt to various situations, is sociable, conscientious, tactful, considerate, and open to various points of view.

The Critical Points in the Chapter that Lead to the Discovery of the Five Definitive Keys to Organizational Success and Sustainability

Critical Point 1

The Personality characteristics of the right type of leader include: an individual who can easily adapt to various situations, is sociable, conscientious, tactful, considerate, and open to various points of view.

References

Cattell, R. B. (July 1973). Personality pinned down. *Psychology Today*, 40–46.

Gordon, J. R. (1996). *Organizational behavior* (5th ed.). Upper Saddle River, NJ: Prentice-Hall.

Hellriegel, D., Slocum J., & Woodman, R. (1995). *Organizational behavior* (7th ed.). St. Paul, MN: West.

Moorhead, G., & Griffin, R. W. (1995). *Organizational behavior: Managing people & organizations* (4th ed.). Boston: Houghton Mifflin.

Robbins, S. (2001). *Organizational behavior* (9th ed.). Upper Saddle River, NJ: Prentice-Hall.

Rotter, J. B. (1966). Generalized expectancies for internal versus external control of reinforcement. *Psychological Monographs, 80*(1), 1–28.

Weber, A. L. (1991). *Introduction to psychology*. New York: Harper Collins.

6

Environmental Factors That Influence "Who We Are"

To a large extent people behave the way they do because of the social situation in which they find themselves.

—Coser, Nock, Steffan, and Spain (1991, p. 4)

Environmental factors that influence our behavior revolve around the cultural environment that an individual is exposed to. Think of a cultural environment as a kaleidoscope of societal elements that swirl around absorbing and influencing every individual caught within its grasp—like the twisting winds of a tornado scooping up everything in its path. Specifically, a cultural environment consists of the attitudes and perspectives shared by a group of individuals, meaning that a unique society has been formed, as well as any subcultures that might exist.

Besides being molded by the societal fingers of the culture in which we live the events of daily life also leave a unique mark upon who we are and how we behave. In fact, the combination of culture and life experi-

Organizational Performance in a Nutshell, pages 33–35

ences such as our family environment, the location(s) where we grew up, the schools we attended, the work situations we encountered, our love relationships and the friends we have chosen are probably responsible for approximately 50% of our personality.

For some individuals the experiences of daily life have left them bitter and viewing the world as a hostile, empty, and foreboding place while for others the opposite is true. What's important for us to remember is that each of us must be aware of our power to positively or negatively impact the outlook of another person. Stopping to offer a few dollars to a homeless person trying to gather enough money to have a meal at McDonald's or helping out at a charitable event may not alter the over-all circumstances of a person who's struggling to survive the harshness of poverty, disease, and homelessness but the fact that an individual is willing to help a less fortunate person speaks a great deal about that individual.

Being able to look beyond our self no matter what circumstances we have encountered in life is a critical quality of the right type of leader. For the right type of leader is not interested in him or her self but instead is focused upon the conditions of all those individuals who work for them. By truly caring about the employees, the right type of leader will achieve unparalleled organizational success.

The Critical Points in the Chapter that Lead to the Discovery of the Five Definitive Keys to Organizational Success and Sustainability

Critical Point 1

The combination of culture and life experiences such as our family environment, the location(s) where we grew up, the schools we attended, the work situations we encountered, our love relationships and the friends we have chosen are probably responsible for approximately 50% of our personality.

Critical Point 2

The right type of leader is not interested in him or her self but instead is focused upon the conditions of all those individuals who work for them. By truly caring about the employees, the right type of leader will achieve unparalleled organizational success.

References

Coser, L A., Nock, S. L., Steffan, P. A., & Spain, D. (1991). *Introduction to sociology* (3rd ed.). Orlando, FL: Harcourt Brace Jovanovich.

7

Attitudes and Motivation

Genuine motivation comes from the way people feel they are treated and the witness that management presents. "Pride in work" is the result of "pride in employees."
—Philip B. Crosby (1986, p. 179)

So far in our quest to unmask our "true" essence and in the process discover the right type of leader we have explored perception and personality—including the environmental factors that surround us and impact who we are.

Flowing from our perceptions and personality are the attitudes or opinions we have adopted. Understanding our attitudes brings us another step closer towards revealing our inner being—our soul if you like. As stated by Stephen Laws (1987, p. 86), "A man is what his thoughts are every day." Each of us express our thoughts or opinions about everything ranging from a particular coaching decision during a football game to what we think about another person to the quality or worth of a piece of art. Our opinions or attitudes may or may not be based upon any facts but every attitude is comprised of three components. The cognitive component is the opinion or belief segment of an attitude. The affective component is the feeling or emotional segment of an attitude. The behavioral component is an intention to behave in a certain manner towards someone or something.

Important workplace attitudes include: job satisfaction, job involvement, and organizational commitment. An individual with a high level of job satisfaction and job involvement has a positive attitude towards the job and strongly identifies with and cares about the kind of work they do. Individuals with a high level of job satisfaction and job involvement tend to also have a high regard for the organization in terms of loyalty, identification, and organizational involvement (Robbins, 2001)

A high level of job satisfaction, job involvement, and organizational commitment stems from matching the physical and intellectual abilities of an employee with the job. When trying to match the abilities of an employee to the job it's critical that we understand the characteristics of the job and a useful tool for accomplishing that is the job characteristics model (JCM). According to the JCM model every job has five core dimensions (skill variety, task identify, task significance, autonomy, and feedback). Skill variety is the degree to which the job requires a variety of different activities. Task identify is the degree to which the job requires completion of a whole and identifiable piece of work. Task significance is the degree to which the job has a substantial impact on the lives or work of other people. Autonomy is the degree to which the job provides substantial freedom and discretion to the individual in scheduling the work and in determining the procedures to be used in carrying it out. Feedback is the degree to which carrying out the work activities results in the individual obtaining feedback about the effectiveness of his or her performance.

When employees are well suited for the job remarkable levels of productivity can be achieved and make no mistake about it, productivity is the key to economic and organizational success:

> Only rising productivity can raise standards of living in the long run. Over long periods of time, small differences in rates of productivity growth compound like interest in a bank account and can make an enormous difference to a society's prosperity. Nothing contributes more to material well-being, to the reduction of poverty, to increases in leisure time, and to a country's ability to finance education, public health, environmental improvement, and the arts than its productivity growth rate. (Baumol & Blinder, 2006)

Productive employees are motivated employees. Motivation refers to an individual's willingness to exert high levels of effort. Employees are willing and able to exert a high level of effort when the employee ability—job match is in equilibrium, when recognition is provided for accomplishments and when opportunities for advancement are available for those employees who desire that. A motivated workforce sets the stage for organizational success and sustainability.

In today's extremely competitive and global business environment no organization can expect to succeed without a highly motivated workforce:

> Social exchange theory posits that individuals form relationships with those who can provide valued resources. In exchange for these resources, individuals will reciprocate by providing resources and support. Thus, individuals will exhibit greater commitment to an organization when they feel supported and rewarded. This commitment, in turn, manifests itself in increased performance and other work behaviors that benefit the organization. (Gouldner, Rhoades, Eisenberger, & Armeli cited by Umbach, 2007, p. 93)

Making a "true" commitment to the employees is what separates the right type of leader from the rest and it's that commitment that inspires the employees to want to accomplish organizational goals in the most efficient and effective manner. In other words, the right type of leader can motivate and lead others towards achieving extraordinary organizational results.

The Critical Points in the Chapter that Lead to the Discovery of the Five Definitive Keys to Organizational Success and Sustainability

Critical Point 1

Employees with a high level of job satisfaction and job involvement tend to also have a high regard for the organization

Critical Point 2

A high level of job satisfaction, job involvement, and organizational commitment stems from matching the physical and intellectual abilities of an employee with the job

Critical Point 3

The Job Characteristics Model (JCM) can be utilized to understand the dimensions of a job.

Critical Point 4

When employees are well suited for the job remarkable gains in productivity can be achieved and make no mistake about it, productivity is the key to economic and organizational success.

Critical Point 5

Productive employees are motivated employees. Motivation is the willingness of an individual to exert high levels of effort. Employees are willing and able to exert a high level of effort when the employee ability—job match is in equilibrium, when recognition is provided for accomplishments and when opportunities for advancement are available for those employees who desire that.

Critical Point 6

Social exchange theory posits that individuals will exhibit greater commitment to an organization when they feel supported and rewarded.

Critical Point 7

Making a "true" commitment to the employees is what separates the right type of leader from the rest and it's that commitment that inspires the employees to want to accomplish organizational goals in the most efficient and effective manner. In other words, the right type of leader can motivate and lead others towards achieving extraordinary organizational results.

References

Baumol, W. J., & Blinder, A. S. (2006). *Economics: Principles and policy* (10th ed.). Mason, OH: Thomson/South-Western.

Crosby, P. B. (1986). *Running things: The art of making things happen.* New York: Mentor.

Hackman, J. R., & Oldham, G. R. (August 1976). Motivation through the design of work: Test of a theory. *Organizational Behavior and Human Performance, 16, 250–279.*

Laws, S. (1987). *The wyrm.* New York: Leisure Books.

Robbins, S. (2001). *Organizational behavior* (9th ed.). Upper Saddle River, NJ: Prentice-Hall.

Umback, P. D. (Winter 2007). How effective are they? Exploring the impact of contingent faculty on undergraduate education. *The Review of Higher Education, 30*(2), 91–123.

8

Do You Want to See?

People fascinate me. Why they do what they do. What makes them tick.
        —Erica Spindler (2001, p. 124)

Do you want to see what makes you tick?

> Maybe it's our free will misdirected or just a shameful pride, but we live our lives with the conviction that we stand at the center of the drama. Moments rarely come that put us outside ourselves, that divorce us from our egos and force us to see the larger picture, to recognize that the drama is in fact a tapestry and each of us is but a thread in the vivid weave, yet each thread essential to the integrity of the cloth. (Koontz, 2004, p. 343)

Self-discovery involves taking an internal peek at something we may not want to see and risk the possibility that we might need to change. Every human being has a perceived image of who they think they are and any challenge to that belief is not something anyone of us tends to welcome. However, personal growth cannot occur unless we objectively journey into our

Organizational Performance in a Nutshell, pages 41–43

41

psyche and thoroughly examine what makes us tick. As stated by Swimme & Berry (1992), "The story of the human is the story of the emergence and development of this self-awareness and its role within the universe drama" (p. 143).

Recall from a previous chapter, the essence of our inner being can be referred to as our self-concept. Our self-concept is an organization or patterning of attitudes, habits, knowledge, drives, and the like, all of which blends together to form our personality. Generally, we reflect upon our self-concept as a result of some circumstances or one's own conscious introspection. This "self-examination is a preparation for insight—a groundbreaking for the seeds of self-understanding that gradually blooms into changed behavior" (Brouwer, 1964). If during the self-examination an individual sees himself (or herself) in a particular respect that he (or she) does not like, then that individual is changing their self-expectation. From a change in self-expectation a new self-concept emerges—like a newborn hatchling breaking through the shell to experience the outside world for the first time. The change in self-concept must ultimately be self-directed—the individual must want to change. In the final analysis, an individual is the master of their own destiny in the sense that the individual takes charge of their personal development. Nothing can be done to an individual to make him (or her) want to grow—an individual matures only if that person has the desire and wherewithal to do so (Brouwer, 1964).

For many people, an internal voyage to the deepest regions of their self-concept may never occur, but for us the path that we have been following has been leading us towards gaining an understanding of who we are and in the process discovering the right type of leader.

Looking beyond the mirror in order to see our true identity is one of the most difficult challenges that a person can encounter in life but as a character in a book by Tamara Thorne (2004) stated "I guess my point is that there's never been a time when I didn't live for information, and I've always felt that, for me at least, learning and growing is the primary purpose of life" (p. 302).

The ultimate quest for knowledge is discovering who we are. Don't be afraid to look and see.

The Critical Points in the Chapter that Lead to the Discovery of the Five Definitive Keys to Organizational Success and Sustainability

Critical Point 1

A journey of self-discovery means risking a peek at something we may not want to see; but in the final analysis life is all about seeing, learning and growing.

References

Brouwer, P. J. (November–December 1964). The power to see ourselves. *Harvard Business Review, 42*(6), 156–165.

Koontz, D. (2004). *Life expectancy.* New York: Bantam Book.

Spindler, E. (2001). *Bone cold.* Don Mills, Ontario: MIRA Books.

Swimme, B., & Berry, T. (1992). *The universe story: From the primordial flaring forth to the ecozoic era—A celebration of the unfolding of the cosmos.* New York: HarperCollins.

Thorne, T. (2004). *Thunder road.* New York: Kensington/Pinnacle Books.

9

Change and Decision-Making

Change means leaving "what we are" and becoming "what we are not.
—Barott & Raybould (1998)

...She was finally coming to her own crossroads. A decision would have to be made.
—Stephen Laws (1987, p. 14)

In the book titled *At Home in Mitford* (Karon, 1996, p. 49), the town doctor is talking with Father Tim about the need to change his lifestyle.

> "This," said Dr. Walter Harper, who was known to the village as Hoppy, "is where the rubber hits the road."
>
> "Meaning?"
>
> "Meaning the party's over, pal. You've got to make some changes, big time."
>
> He sighed. Change! If there was anything he didn't like, that was it, right there in a nutshell.

Organizational Performance in a Nutshell, pages 45–50
Copyright © 2009 by Information Age Publishing

Resistance to change casts blinders over a person leaving that individual unable to see who they really are. As a species, human beings tend to resist change for several reasons.

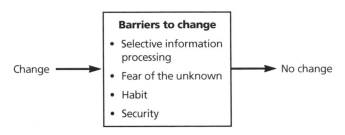

Selective information processing refers to our perception of the environment in which we live and once we have created our outlook of the world any attempt to alter that view meets with resistance. We selectively process the information that flows to us from the environment in order to maintain our perspective of reality. We see what we want to see, we hear what we want to hear, we interpret situations according to our perceptions and so forth. Selective information processing provides an individual with shelter from a changing world

Fear of the unknown is a powerful emotion that causes us to prefer our present condition (no matter how uncomfortable it may be) to a new, uncertain situation. In the book titled *Who Moved My Cheese?* (Johnson, 1998)—Hem cannot leave "Cheese Station C" even though that situation is turning bleaker and bleaker with every passing moment.

Habits as defined by Stephen Covey (1989) consist of three overlapping internalized principles knowledge (what to, why to), skills (how to) and desire (want to). These principles combine to form our pattern of behavior. "By working on knowledge, skill, and desire, we can break through to new levels of personal and interpersonal effectiveness as we break with old paradigms that may have been a source of pseudo-security for years" (Covey, 1989, pp. 47–48). However, Covey goes on to point out that the process of improving our personal and interpersonal effectiveness is sometimes a painful process that many of us sly away from.

Individuals that have a high need for security tend to resist change more than risk taking individuals. Risk-takers thrive on change and seek out the unknown and are not intimidated by what change might bring while individuals longing for security hide from change always seeking stability and consistency.

Change can bring about economic fears in terms of income and established work tasks, routines and patterns. In a work environment, an individual may be concerned about their ability to perform a new task especially when one's pay is directly related to how productive that individual is in performing that new task.

Resisting change strikes a fatal blow to an objective self-examination leaving us alone in the dark no longer capable of searching for our true identity and subsequently unable to continue our quest towards discovering the right type of leader. To avoid the darkness we must never forget that:

> Life is a journey... and as with any journey, a traveler will come upon unexpected twists and turns. Sometimes a person will follow the same path for so long that change seems imperceptible. Conversely, another will travel the shortest of distances and discover a completely new landscape. In a single lifetime, it is possible to live both experiences... (Macomber, 2005)

The right type of leader embraces change, whether it is small or large; when ever it is necessary to do so. In fact the right type of leader actively promotes an organizational culture that has an enhanced capacity to learn, adapt, and change.

From an organizational perspective, three types of change have been identified (Schlechty, 1997). Procedural change is an alteration in the order in which events occur, the pace in which they occur, or the configuration of events. In short, procedural change involves process changes. Technological changes occur because of advancements in technology. Systemic change involves changes in beliefs, values, rules, relationships, and orientation or in other words, a change in the culture of the organization.

Each of the three types of organizational changes is comprised of six underlying characteristics (Hord, Rutherford, Huling-Austin, & Hall, 1987). The first characteristic is that change should be viewed as a process that occurs over a period of time; change is not a single event. The second characteristic is that change is accomplished through the efforts of specific individuals not groups or programs. The third characteristic is that each person in the organization may react to the change in a unique way. The fourth characteristic is that as individuals begin to trust and respect the new practice, they begin to grow in their desire and ability to use it. The fifth characteristic is that an individual will react to change in terms of how it impacts their work situation. The final characteristic is that people institute change and the focus should be upon the people who are going to implement the change as well as those who will be impacted by it.

The bottom line regarding organizational or personal change is that to change means to alter a paradigm. Frazier cited by Zepeda (1999) defined a paradigm as "powerful expressions of how each of us perceives, understands and interprets our environments and our relationships with individuals and organizations" (p. 122). In order for each of us to achieve a higher level of personal growth and maturity we must be willing to come to grips with the fact that some (or maybe all) of the paradigms we hold as gospel may need to be changed. The issue now becomes a question of what decision do you want to make? Are you willing to objectively analyze yourself and change, if necessary?

I believe Charles Pellegrino (1988) summarized life in the following manner. When it's all said and done about life, the only thing we can truly call our own are the decisions we have made. For those individuals who are still not completely sure that they want to see beyond their public persona then this is probably the time to put the book aside until the time is right for you to continue the journey. For those who want to see the next chapter will provide a framework for understanding who you are and in the process discover the right type of leader.

The Critical Point in the Chapter that Lead to the Discovery of the Five Definite Keys to Organizational Success and Sustainability

Critical Point 1

Barriers to change include: selective information processing, fear of the unknown, habit, and security.

Critical Point 2

Resisting change strikes a fatal blow to an objective self-examination leaving us alone in the dark no longer capable of searching for our true identity and subsequently unable to continue our quest towards discovering the right type of leader.

Critical Point 3

The right type of leader embraces change, whether it is small or large; when ever it is necessary to do so. In fact the right type of leader actively promotes an organizational culture that has an enhanced capacity to learn, adapt, and change.

Critical Point 4

From an organizational perspective, three types of change have been identified: procedural, technological, and systemic.

Critical Point 5

Each of the three types of organizational changes is comprised of six underlying characteristics. Change is: (a) a process, (b) accomplished by individuals, not groups or programs, (c) a highly personal experience, (d) incremental, (e) understand best in terms of one's own practice, and (f) accomplished by focusing upon the individuals involved in the implementation (Zepeda, 1999).

Critical Point 6

The bottom line regarding change, whether it is organizational or personal, is that to change means to alter a paradigm.

Critical Point 7

In order for each of us to achieve a higher level of personal growth and maturity we must be willing to make the decision that the paradigms we hold as gospel may need to be changed.

Critical Point 8

The issue now becomes a question of what decision do you want to make? Do you want to take the last step in our journey to discover who you truly are and in the process discover the right type of leader?

References

Barott, J., & Raybould, R. (1998). Changing schools into collaborative organizations. In D. G. Pounder (Ed.), *Restructuring schools for collaboration: Promises and pitfalls* (pp. 27–42). Albany: State University of New York Press.

Brouwer, P. J. (November–December 1964). The power to see ourselves. *Harvard Business Review, 42*(6), 156–165.

Covey, S. R. (1989). *The 7 habits of highly effective people.* New York: Fireside Books.

Frazier, A. (1997). *A roadmap for quality transformation in education.* Boca Raton, FL: St. Lucie Press.

Hord, S., Rutherford, W., Huling-Austin, L., & Hall, G. (1987). *Taking charge of change.* Alexandria, VA: Association for Supervision and Curriculum.

Johnson, S. (1998). *Who moved my cheese?* New York: G. P. Putnam's Sons.

Karon, J. (1996). *At home in Mitford.* New York: Penguin Books.

Laws, S. (1987). *The wyrm.* New York: Leisure Books.

Macomber, D. (2005). *There's something about Christmas.* Don Mills, Ontario, Canada: MIRA Books.

Pellegrino, C. (1988). *Her name, Titanic.* New York: Avon Books.

Schlechty, P. (1997). *Inventing better schools.* San Francisco, CA: Jossey-Bass.

Zepeda, S. J. (1999). *Staff development: Practices that promote leadership in learning communities.* Larchmont, NY: Eye on Education.

10

Two Approaches to Life and Management

The Right Leader

Ego is an incredibly serious problem.
—Philip B. Crosby (1986, p. 157)

$\mathbf{A}$t the end of the movie *High Plains Drifter*, as the leader of a notorious band of outlaws is frantically looking from side to side in the hope of spotting a fast shooting, mysterious drifter, the villain shouts in a desperate, haunting tone "Who are you?" As sweat drips down the face of the outlaw and fear fills his eyes, the only response from the drifter is a bullet that ends the villain's life upon this Earth. Hell is the next stop for the outlaw and quite possibly for the mysterious drifter too.

Fortunately for us, in our quest of self-discovery we have not had to engage in a violent struggle between the forces of good and evil; and the middle ground between those two extremes; but we have had to wrestle with the concepts of perception, personality, attitudes and motivation. It's the mixing together of those concepts that mold us into who we are—just

Organizational Performance in a Nutshell, pages 51–59
51

like a sculptor chisels upon a piece of marble until the desired form is achieved. The end result for the sculptor is a work of art. The final outcome for an individual is the development of a particular approach to life. Every human being tends to view life from one of two perspectives. These two perspectives or approaches to life not only define who we truly are but also guide us towards an understanding of what it takes to be the right type of leader; since the right type of leader can only emerge from one of the two approaches to life.

Understanding "Who We Are" and in the Process Discovering the Right Type of Leader

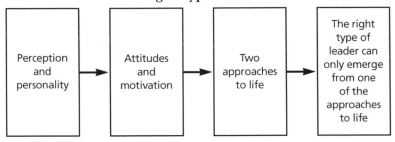

Let's consider two individuals. The first person is (a) highly materialistic; (b) always focused upon their needs; (c) not concerned about how goals are achieved as long as they are accomplished; (d) only concerned with the here and now; (e) insensitive towards the physical environment; meaning at the macro level, the Earth and at the micro level, the workplace; (f) not interested in anyone else's point of view; (g) power driven; and finally (h) constantly favoring certain individuals. The second person has the opposite characteristics.

Which individual would you prefer as a boss? I don't believe anyone of us would select the first individual and if you were unfortunate enough to have to work for that type of person how much effort would you put forth? The first individual has the characteristics associated with an egocentric view of life. The second person has adopted an altruistic view of life. The right type of leader must possess an altruistic perspective of life for only that kind of person will have the characteristics that are necessary to inspire others to want to do their best.

An egocentric person is primarily consumed with satisfying their needs. An altruistic person focuses upon the interests of others and as a result gains the trust and loyalty of those who work for them. It is that bond of trust and loyalty between the altruistic leader and the employees that sets the foundation for obtaining extraordinary organizational results. Put simply, in terms of achieving organizational success and sustainability an individual with an egocentric approach to life will in the long run never measure up to a person with an altruistic viewpoint.

Understanding Who We Are and in the Process Discovering the Right Type of Leader

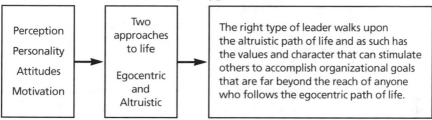

| Perception Personality Attitudes Motivation | Two approaches to life Egocentric and Altruistic | The right type of leader walks upon the altruistic path of life and as such has the values and character that can stimulate others to accomplish organizational goals that are far beyond the reach of anyone who follows the egocentric path of life. |

Given the importance of leadership—what exactly is it? Unfortunately a straightforward definition has proven allusive for leadership has been defined by many individuals in many ways:

- Leadership is both a process and a property. As a process, leadership involves the use of non-coercive influences. As a property, leadership is the set of characteristics attributed to someone who is perceived to use influence successfully (Moorhead & Griffin, 1995)
- Leadership is the process whereby one person influences others to work toward a goal and helps them pursue a vision (Yulk and VanFleet cited by Hellriegel, Slocum, & Woodman, 1995)
- Leadership is the process of guiding and motivating others toward the achievement of organizational goals (Gitman & McDaniel, 2003)
- Leadership is first figuring out what's right, and then explaining it to people; as opposed to first having people explain to you what's right, and then just saying what they want to hear (Judy Giuliani)
- Strategic leadership refers to the ability to articulate a strategic vision for the company, or a part of the company, and to motivate others to buy into that vision (Hill & Jones, 1998)

- Leadership is the ability to influence a group toward the achievement of goals (Robbins, 2001)
- Leadership ... is the ability to get other people to get the very best out of themselves. And it is manifested ... not by getting them to follow you, but by getting them to join you. You don't get the best out of people by bulldozing them; you do it by educating (or convincing) them (Marv Levy, 2004)
- Leadership is the ability to decide what is to be done, and then to get others to do it (Dwight Eisenhower)
- Leadership requires distinct behaviors and attitudes. ... When you become a leader, success is all about growing others (Jack Welch)

And the list can go on and on, but in the end, the definition isn't important what matters is that you are the right type of leader meaning an individual who pursues organizational goals and objectives in such a way that the growth and integrity of people are respected (Johnston cited by Seyfarth, 1999). The specific characteristics of the right type of leader which have already been cited in the book include:

- The right type of leader has the right self-image and self-concept to want to create a workplace in which the traditional management-employee relationship paradigm is cast aside in favor of the new management-employee paradigm meaning that employees are regarded as partners not subordinates; in other words management must put employees first—and mean it. Management retains the final decision-making authority but the focus should be upon how an organizational decision impacts the employees for that in turn will influence how the employees perform their job and ultimately how they interact with the customer.
- The right type of leader can easily adapt to various situations, is sociable, conscientious, tactful, considerate, and open to various points of view
- The right type of leader is not interested in him or her self but instead is focused upon the conditions of all those individuals who work for them. By truly caring about the employees, the right type of leader will achieve unparalleled organizational success. In other words, the right type of leader makes a true commitment to the employees and it's that commitment that inspires the employees to want to accomplish organizational goals in the most effective and efficient manner (social exchange theory).

- The right type of leader embraces change, whether it is small or large, whenever it is necessary to do so. In fact the right type of leader actively promotes an organizational culture that has an enhanced capacity to learn, adapt, and change.
- The right type of leader must possess an altruistic perspective of life for only that kind of person has the characteristics to inspire others to want to do their best
- The right type of leader pursues organizational goals and objectives in such a way that the growth and integrity of people are respected.

Now let's compare the characteristics of the right type of leader with a leadership style that flows from an egocentric perspective of life and can best be described as a CREEP approach to leadership:

- CREEPS are *control* freaks. A CREEP makes all the decisions and only makes a token or superficial effort to seek employee input or suggestions. CREEPS are the ultimate micro-managers. Anything not initiated by the CREEP is rejected.
- CREEPS form *relationships* with favorite employees; work performance is secondary. Only those in the inner circle of the CREEP are allowed any involvement in the day-to-day managerial activities of the organization.
- CREEPS have king or queen size *egos* and view employees as cogs in a machine that can be easily replaced. CREEPS have none or very little concern for employees except for the CREEPS favorite employees. CREEPS utilize HR policies to intimidate and severely limit employee empowerment.
- CREEPS have limited *ethics*. CREEPS utilize a Machiavellian approach to getting tasks accomplished. CREEPS are abusive and manipulative. CREEPS are only concerned about them self and view others as human pawns that can be used as the CREEP sees fit—any employee development will only occur if it benefits the CREEP.
- CREEPS love *power* and institute a top-down managerial philosophy. CREEPS are not interested in developing future leaders for those individuals are viewed by CREEPS as threats. CREEPS love to show off their power.
- CREEPS are as *secretive* as possible. CREEPS don't like to share information with employees. Employees find out information through the grapevine. When a CREEP does have to share

information with employees it's communicated through formal communication channels and generally the employees are not allowed (or only superficially allowed) to be part of the decision-making process.

The difference between the right type of leader and a CREEP can also be illustrated by slightly modifying the work of Peters and Austin (1985). A description of the right type of leader includes:

- Comfortable with people
- Puts employees first
- Open-door cheerleader
- No reserved parking place, private washroom, or dining room
- Common touch
- Good listener
- Fair
- Humble
- Tough, confronts nasty problems
- Tolerant of disagreement (respectful of the opinion of others)
- Has strong convictions (altruistic approach to life)
- Trusts people
- Gives credit, takes blame
- Prefers personal communication to written communication such as memos, email or long reports
- Keeps promises
- Thinks there are at least two other people in the organization who would be good CEOs

The description of a CREEP is as follows:

- Uncomfortable with people
- Puts their needs first, not the needs of the employees
- Generally inaccessible to employees
- Has a reserved parking place, private washroom, and dining area
- Strained relationship with employees
- Good talker in terms of outlining what they want, poor listener
- Fair to their favorite employees, exploit the rest
- Arrogant
- Avoid nasty problems, elusive, the artful dodger
- Intolerant of disagreement, does not respect the opinion of others
- No firm stand, vacillates and utilizes a Machiavellian approach

- Distrusts employees and focuses upon numbers on reports
- Takes credit, blames others for failures
- Prefer written communication to personal contact
- Does not keep promises
- Makes sure that no one is hired who remotely resembles a CEO (or a challenge to their authority)

In terms of organizational performance which leadership style will achieve maximum performance? I think it's quite obvious that the right type of leader can create a workplace characterized by highly energized and productive employees willing to do what ever it takes to satisfy the customer. A CREEP leadership style will establish an organizational environment in which minimum performance is the norm.

An organization with the right type of leaders will out perform an organization filled with CREEPS because the right type of leaders can tap the full potential of the workforce. Thus the first definitive key to organizational success and sustainability is to fill organizational leadership positions with the right type of leaders—meaning individuals who possess an altruistic approach to life and focus upon the needs of the employees. CREEPS must be eliminated from leadership or managerial positions.

The First Definite Key to Organizational Success and Sustainability

Fill organizational leadership positions with the right type of leaders—meaning individuals who possess the "right type of leader" characteristics described in the chapter. CREEPS must be eliminated from any leadership or managerial position.

Leadership and organizational success and sustainability are forever locked in an eternal struggle against the numerous forces in today's highly competitive marketplace that can devour an organization at any moment. The critical role of leadership can best be summarized by the following story that was told by Dr. Ronald Walker (2007) during a class that I was taking at Jackson State University:

> You can learn a lot about leadership by watching a farmer trying to get a group of cows to move from one pasture to another. The farmer can get behind the cows and try to push them through one gate and into another. Eventually the farmer will get the cows into the next pasture however he would have spent a lot of time and used a lot of effort in the process. Instead of trying to push the

cows, the farmer could have observed which cow was the lead cow and place a bucket of feed in front of that cow and easily, with minimum effort, lead that cow, and subsequently the other cows, out of one gate and through another into a new pasture. However, what we must always be careful of is who has the bucket and where are they leading us? It could be to the slaughterhouse.

With the right type of leader no one needs to worry about the direction in which the organization is heading for that decision would have been mutually agreeable upon between management and the employees. Ultimately it's the values and character of the right type of leader which are grounded within an altruistic approach to life that will allow for the creation of a productive workplace characterized by motivated employees who are always willing to do their best for the customer. That's the kind of organization that will survive the rigors of the marketplace and achieve sustainability.

The Critical Points in the Chapter that Lead to the Discovery of the Five Definitive Keys to Organizational Success and Sustainability

Critical Point 1

The right type of leader can only emerge from an altruistic approach to life.

Critical Point 2

The right type of leader focuses upon the needs of the employees thereby creating a workplace characterized by highly motivated and productive employees who are focused upon satisfying the needs of the customer. In other words, the right type of leader pursues organizational goals and objectives in such a way that the growth and integrity of people are respected. Other characteristics of the right type of leader include: comfortable with people; puts employees first; open-door cheerleader; no reserved parking place, private washroom, or dining room; common touch; good listener; fair; humble; tough, confronts nasty problems; tolerant of disagreement (respectful of the opinion of others); has strong convictions (altruistic approach to life); trusts people; gives credit, takes blame; prefers personal communication over written communication such as memos, email or long reports; keeps promises; and thinks there are at least two other people in the organization who would be good CEOs.

Critical Point 3

CREEPS must always be eliminated from any management or leadership position.

Critical Point 4

The first definitive key to organizational success and sustainability is embodied in the first, three critical points of this chapter

References

Bateman, T., & Zeithaml, C. (1990). *Management: Function and strategy.* Homewood, IL: Richard D. Irwin, p. 504

Carney, B. M. (2007, June 30–July 1). Of tax cuts and terror. *The Wall Street Journal,* p. A7.

Crosby, P. B. (1986). *Running things: The art of making things happen.* New York: Mentor.

Gitman, L. J., & McDaniel, C. (2003) *The best of the future of business.* Mason, OH: Thomson/South-Western.

Hellriegel D., Slocum, J., & Woodman, R. (1995). *Organizational behavior* (7th ed.). St. Paul, MN: West.

Hill, C. W. L., & Jones, G. R. (1998). *Strategic management: An integrated approach.* Boston, MA: Houghton Mifflin.

Levy, M. (2004). *Where else would you rather be?* Champaign, IL: Sports.

Moorhead, G., & Griffin, R. W. (1995). *Organizational behavior: Managing people & organizations* (4th ed.). Boston: Houghton Mifflin.

Peters, T., & Austin, N. (1985). *A passion for excellence.* New York: Random House.

Robbins, S. (2001). *Organizational behavior* (9th ed.). Upper Saddle River, NJ: Prentice-Hall.

Seyfarth, J. T. (1999). *The principal: New leadership for new challenges.* Upper Saddle River, NJ: Prentice-Hall.

Walker, R. (Spring 2007). Class lecture at Jackson State University.

Welch, J., & Welch S. (2005, April 4). How to be a good leader. *Newsweek,* pp. 45–48.

PART **3**

Group and Organizational Dynamics

11

The Forces Influencing Group Performance

When a group of individuals become a "we," a harmonious whole,
then the highest is reached that humans as creatures can reach.

—Albert Einstein

"**W**hat was it about the darkness? It could the idea of the unknown, always lying hidden in the dark" (Graham, 2007, p. 129). As we continue navigating through the darkness that shrouds the answers to organizational sustainability our next step must take us beyond the search for the right leader. In discovering the first definite key to organizational success we learned that the right leader is an individual who possesses the personal characteristics and managerial attitude that is necessary to establish a work environment where the employees want to assert a maximum effort to satisfy customer needs. As stated by Michael Fullan (2007) "the litmus test of all leadership is whether it mobilizes peoples' commitment to putting their energy into actions designed to improve things. It is individual commitment, but above all it is collective mobilization" (p. 9).

Organizational Performance in a Nutshell, pages 63–69
Copyright © 2009 by Information Age Publishing
All rights of reproduction in any form reserved.

Finding the second definite key to organizational success and sustainability will require us move to travel through a very different terrain, that of group performance, or maximizing the collective efforts of the members within an organization. In most workplaces individuals cannot work alone to satisfy customer needs and accomplish organizational goals. Generally organizational accomplishments are achieved at the group or department level. The importance of group productivity can be highlighted by the fact that year in and year out business executives have consistently requested that business school graduates be able to function effectively and efficiently in a group setting. The State University of New York at Buffalo, a university that I earned a degree in economics from, has been continually cited as a leading university in terms of developing individuals who work well in groups.

To illustrate the critical nature of individuals working together as a productive group let's once again consider an orchestra. Despite the talent of each musician if they are not playing the same notes at the same time the sound emulating from the orchestra will not be a pleasant one. In order to create beautiful music every musician must be on the same page working together as a harmonious whole. It is the group effort that spells success and satisfies the needs of the customer.

From a strict business perspective, if the marketing department and the production department are not working together what are the chances of producing a product that will satisfy customer wants? I think we all know the answer to that question. By the way have you ever had the unpleasant task of working for an organization where different departments were on totally different pages in terms of product development, production, marketing, and so forth? I don't you about you, but I have heard stories from many people who have worked at organizations where the right hand did not know (or in many cases did not care) what the left hand was doing. How does that impact group performance and customer satisfaction?

Maximizing group performance is as critical as maximizing individual performance. However, before venturing further into the realm of group performance lets consider the over-all question of why is an individual willing to become part of a group. The research into this question can be summarized by the following reasons: (a) security, (b) status, (c) self-esteem, (d) affiliation, (e) power, and finally (f) goal achievement. In a work environment all or some of these explanations may be appropriate and could serve as the foundation for the purpose of the group. However, another factor needs to be considered when examining formal groups in an organizational setting and that factor is how are formal work groups designed and defined by the organization's structure. Two specific types of formal work groups are a command group and a task group. A command group includes the manager and his or her immediate subordinates. A task group consists of two or more individuals working together to complete a task. A task group's organizational boundaries may reach beyond its immediate hierarchical structure, in other words, a task group can cut across organizational hierarchical structures; for a command group this may or may not be the case. However all command groups are task groups. For our purposes, we'll use the term, department, to include the notion of a command and task group.

Since a department is a subsystem within a larger system (an organization) a good starting point for understanding how to effectively and efficiently manage a department is to examine systems theory. Simply stated, a *system* is a group of interrelated or interacting elements forming a unified whole that works toward a common goal by accepting inputs and producing outputs in an organized transformation process. A dynamic system essentially has three basic interacting components or functions: an input function that involves capturing and assembling elements that enter the system to be processed; a processing element or transformation process that converts an input into an output; and the output that has been produced. A cybernetic system includes two additional components: feedback and control. *Feedback* is the data about the performance of a system. *Control* involves monitoring and evaluating feedback to determine whether or not a system is moving toward the achievement of its goal(s). In addition, a system can either be classified as an open system or an adaptive system. An *open system* is a system that interacts with other systems in its environment. An *adaptive system* has the ability to change itself or its environment in order to survive.

Every system has all three components: input, processing, and output. An effective and efficient system has all five system components working together as a harmonious whole—these three, as well as feedback and control. Thus, systems theory provides a meaningful methodology for examining the workings of a department as it operates within the managerial and structural boundaries of the organization.

Another framework for conceptualizing what constitutes a system is provided by Patrick Morley (2001) in his book *Coming Back to God*. "The 'collection' of ideas we embrace forms a system that guides our choices, and hence shapes the course of our future" (p. 76). Here's the problem: if the 'system' you build will not work, you may not know it doesn't work until a substantial period of time passes. "By then, damage is done and you will have given the best years of your life to a system that has failed you" (p. 76).

Morley's main point is that systems are designed to produce the results or outcomes that are occurring, whether those outcomes are positive or negative. From an organizational perspective, what can be learned from Morley's ideas? The ramifications are quite clear: if your organization is under-performing, it is the systems that have been established within the organization that are producing those poor results. To correct the situation, those systems must be either modified or abandoned (in which case new systems will need to be developed).

So what system elements impact the success or failure of a department? Those factors are listed below:

1. Organizational conditions imposed on the department
2. Department member resources
3. Department structure
4. Department processes
5. Department task

Organizational conditions imposed on the department include:

- The over-all strategy of the organization. This impacts where organizational resources will be allocated
- The over-all authority structure of the organization. This determines where a particular department falls within the over-all organizational scheme with-in the organization. The organizational hierarchy impacts the formal leadership and the relationship between each department with-in the organization.
- The formal over-all organizational rules, procedures, and policies that standardize decision-making and membership behavior within the organization.
- The organizational culture or the unwritten code of conducts within the organization from which many of the formal rules, procedures, and policies are derived from
- The physical work environment in which tasks are conducted.

Department member resources:

- The knowledge, skills, and abilities of each employee
- The personality characteristics of each employee such as sociability, openness, flexibility, initiative and so forth.

Department structure:

- The leadership style of the department manager
- The set of expected behavior patterns attributed to an individual occupying a given position with-in the department. In other words, the role that each individuals plays with-in the department. For example, in an educational setting, a faculty member may have to play several roles during the course of a day such as being a teacher, a student counselor, a peer advisor, a researcher or writer and so forth. In each role the faculty member is expected to behave in a certain manner as defined by norms of the department.
- Department norms are the acceptable standards of behavior within a department that are shared by the members. Department norms include: (a) performance norms; (b) appearance norms; (c) social arrangement norms which guide social interaction among the group members; (d) allocation of resources; and (e) level of conformity
- The status of the department meaning the socially defined position or rank given to a department or department members by others
- Department size or span of control. Generally speaking, a manager can effectively and efficiently supervise between 7 to 12 direct subordinates.
- Department demographics or diversity. Diverse groups tend to take a longer time to work through disagreements and approaches for solving problems; however the research tend to indicate that these differences become less of a factor after approximately three months. Heterogeneous groups are more likely to have diverse abilities and information and generally speaking are very effective.
- Department cohesiveness refers to the degree to which department members are attracted to each other and are motivated to stay in the department.

Department processes:

- Department processes encompass such activities as (a) communication among department members; (b) department decision-making; (c) power and conflict dynamics with-in the department; and (d) leadership behavior.

Department task:

▪ Tasks can be complex or simple. Complex tasks are novel or non-routine. Simple tasks are routine and standardized.

Maximizing each of the factors that impact department performance will help to maximize organizational performance. Thus understanding how to maximize department performance constitutes the second definitive key to organizational success and sustainability.

Chain of Workplace Activity that Influences Organizational Success and Sustainability

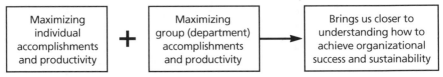

The Critical Points in the Chapter that Lead to the Discovery of the Five Definitive Keys to Organizational Success and Sustainability

Critical Point 1

In most workplaces individuals cannot work alone to satisfy customer needs and accomplish organizational goals. Generally organizational accomplishments are achieved at the group or department level.

Critical Point 2

Groups or departments are impacted by the organizational conditions imposed on the group or department, department member resources, department structure, department processes, and department task.

Critical Point 3

Understanding how to maximize the factors that impact group or department performance constitutes the second definitive key to organizational success and sustainability.

References

Fullan, M. (2007). *Leading in a culture of change* (rev. ed.). San Francisco, CA: Jossey-Bass.

Graham, H. (2007). *The séance,* Don Mills, Ontario, Canada: MIRA Books.

Morley, P. (2001). *Coming back to God.* Grand Rapids, MI: Zondervan.

Robbins, S. (2001). *Organizational behavior* (9th ed.). Upper Saddle River, NJ: Prentice Hall.

12

Putting Employees First and Other Building Blocks of a Great Place to Work

People respond to what is around them.
Philip B. Crosby (1986, p. 179))

The following tale was written by Byham and Cox (1988):

Ralph worked in Dept N of the Normal Company in Normalburg, USA. For years, Normal had been a leading manufacturer of normalators, those amazing devices which are so fundamental to society as we know it.

As you might expect, just about everything was normal at Normal, including the understanding of who was normally supposed to do what:

Managers did the thinking

Supervisors did the talking

And employees did the doing

That was the way it had always been—ever since Norman Norman had invented the normalator and founded the company—and so everybody just assumed that was the way it should always be.

Ralph was your normal type of employee. He came to work. He did the job his supervisor told him to do. And at the end of the day he dragged himself home to get ready to do it all again.

When friends or family asked him how he liked his work, Ralph would say, "Oh, it's all right, I guess. Not very exciting, but I guess that's normal. Anyway, it's a job and the pay is OK."

In truth, working for the Normal Company was not very satisfying for Ralph, though he was not sure why. The pay was more than OK; it was good. The benefits were fine, the working conditions were safe. Yet something seemed to be missing.

But Ralph figured there wasn't much he could do to change things at Normal. After all, he reasoned, who would even bother to listen? So at work he kept his thoughts to himself, and just did what he was told. (pp. 3–4)

Have you ever worked for an organization, like the Normal Company, where it felt like no one cared about you and that your contribution to the organization was always minimized? Unfortunately, I have worked for several organizations like that, with the worse being a situation where senior officials thought they were the greatest things on Earth and the rest of us were there to do their bidding. The message emanating throughout that institution consisted of fear and intimidation. Each employee dreaded every workday, and very few employees went beyond what was required to do their jobs. Just trying to make it to Friday was the fuel that kept you going.

Gaining an insight into the dynamics within an organization and realizing that the culture within an organization can positively or negatively impact workplace performance is nothing new; in fact, it can be traced back to the concept of institutionalization, whereby an organization takes on a life of its own well beyond the original vision of the founder(s).

Institutionalization and organizational culture highlight the importance of fostering a workplace environment in which employees are encouraged to develop innovative and creative ideas, products, services, methods of production and distribution. Understanding how to nourish an innovative and creative environment suitable for maintaining high levels of individual and group productivity revolves around three critical workplace parameters: managerial attitudes and practices in the workplace, the organizational environment among the employees, and the tasks being performed within an organization. These three workplace parameters were identified by Robert Levering (1988) in his book, *A Great Place to Work: What Makes Some Employers So Good (and Most So Bad)*.

Managerial Attitudes and Practices in the Workplace

Managerial attitudes and practices in the workplace can be assessed by the overall degree of trust or lack of trust between administrative and non-administrative personnel. An adversarial relationship between administrative and non-administrative personnel tends to develop when management focuses too much on operational, financial, and marketing issues while ignoring or paying limited attention to the well being of its employees. Dissatisfied employees purposely engage in many behaviors that limit productivity and compromise organizational success. A fertile breeding ground for advancing productivity and promoting organizational success can only be laid when individuals are respected for who they are and placed in positions that complement their strengths.

Gwartney, Stroup, Sobel, and Macpherson (2009) put it this way. "To summarize, institutions and policies matter for economic growth because they shape the incentives individuals confront" (pp. 342–343). As William Baumol has noted and cited by Gwartney, Stroup, Sobel, and Macpherson (2009), "When institutions and policies provide secure property rights, a fair and balanced judicial system, monetary stability, and effective limits on government's ability to transfer wealth through taxation and regulation, creative individuals are more likely to engage in product development, investment, and other productive activities." Organizations or . . . "institutions that encourage productive activities and discourage counterproductive ones will lead to more growth and higher incomes" (pp. 342–343).

From a strict organizational perspective, the right managerial attitude can breathe life into a management philosophy or culture that will boost the chances of organizational success by establishing a workplace environment in which individuals will want to consistently perform at their best. "A social organization premised on equity, security, and participation will generate greater productivity than one premised on greed and fear," Robert Reich wrote in 1983 (pp. 84, 90). Robert Levering (1988) had this to say about organizations where there is trust between administrative and non-administrative personnel: "The dynamic of relentless self-interest is supplanted by a different kind of relationship, where both sides find common ground to work together for their mutual benefit without compromising their separate interests" (Levering, 1988, pp. 83, 84).

The Organizational Environment Among the Employees

The organizational environment among the employees can be assessed by the extent of cooperation and internal politics and favoritism within the organization. A highly politicized work environment will eat away at collegiality and undermine productivity. If left unchecked, it will eventually squelch innovation, cripple productivity, and destroy the organization. The long-term survival of any organization will depend on whether or not it controls internal politics and favoritism. Any organization that fails to base performance and compensation on merit will drift into mediocrity and possibly face extinction in the global marketplace. Merit must be rewarded; favoritism must be discouraged.

The Tasks Being Performed within an Organization

The tasks being performed within an organization can be assessed by asking whether or not a task has meaning for that individual. A recent study of 50,000 employees at 60 organizations found that most employees don't understand how their work contributes to the organization's goals and vision. Individuals tend to be more productive when they sense that their work means something and that they "mean something," and when they feel that their organization is making a positive impact on society. The recent financial scandals regarding Enron, WorldCom, Qwest, HealthSouth, and so forth illustrate the negative impact of an organizational culture that fosters unethical behavior.

A culture of what Alan Greenspan, former chairman of the Federal Reserve, calls "infectious greed" eventually cripples an organization. On the other hand, organizations that create an environment where individuals feel that their work is important and that their organization is providing a positive benefit to the community set the stage for innovation and creativity. When innovation and creativity flourish, so will productivity—the driving force behind economic growth and survival.

Using the three workplace parameters as our base, we lay the foundation to identify four distinct organizational cultures.

Managerial Attitudes and Practices in the Workplace

Individuals tend to trust the administration when operational, financial, marketing, and employee satisfaction issues are given equal attention by management.

Individuals tend to distrust the administration when management focuses on operational, financial, and marketing issues, yet ignores employee satisfaction issues or gives them only limited attention.

The Organizational Environment

The ideal environment is one in which cooperation among individuals and departments/units is encouraged, politicking and favoritism are discouraged, and performance and compensation issues are based on merit.

An atmosphere of non-cooperation exists when cooperation among individuals and departments/units is discouraged, politicking and favoritism are encouraged, and performance and compensation issues are not based on merit.

The Tasks Being Performed Within an Organization

The task has meaning to the individual when he or she feels that his or her actions have a meaningful impact on the organization. The individual should feel that the organization stands for something more than just the pursuit of profits—that it also contributes to the welfare of the community. In addition, the organization must pursue ethical behavior in accomplishing its daily and long-term strategic objectives.

Tasks do not have meaning if individuals feel that their actions have no meaningful impact on the organization, the organization does not stand for something more than just the pursuit of profits, and the organization encourages a culture of infectious greed.

With our measurement criteria established, we can now see four distinct organizational cultures:

Organizational Culture A:
- There is a relationship of trust between administrative and non-administrative personnel.
- Cooperation between individuals and departments/units is encouraged and politicking and favoritism are discouraged.
- Individuals feel that their actions have a meaningful impact on the organization. That their organization stands for more than just the pursuit of profits and its policies are based upon ethical behavior and practices.

Organizational Culture B:
- Two of the three elements of organizational culture "A" are present (e.g., trust and cooperation). However, the tasks might not have meaning for the individual.

Organizational Culture D:

- One of the three elements of organizational culture "A" is present (e.g., the tasks might have meaning for the individual, but there is no trust or cooperation present within the culture of the organization).

Organizational Culture F:

- None of the three elements of organizational culture "A" are present.

Now that we have identified four measurable and distinct organizational cultures, we can present the financial status model of organizational culture (FSMOC) that can be utilized to illustrate the financial performance of an organization based upon its culture, *ceteris paribus.*

The Financial Status Model of Organizational Culture (FSMOC)

Measurement criteria	Financial status of organization	Recommended course of action
Organizational Culture A		
1. Trust 2. Cooperation 3. Task has meaning	Higher financial performance, compared to other organizations within the same industry	Continue present policies and practices
Organizational Culture B		
Two of the three elements of organizational culture "A" are present	Competitive financial performance, compared to other organizations within the same industry	Incorporate the missing element of organizational culture "A" into the "B" culture
Organizational Culture D		
One of the three elements of organizational culture "A" is present	Below-average financial performance, compared to other organizations within the same industry	Incorporate the two missing elements of organizational culture "A" into the "D" culture
Organizational Culture F		
1. Distrust 2. Non-cooperation 3. Task does not have meaning	Significantly below-average financial performance, compared to other organizations within the same industry	Incorporate the three missing elements of organizational culture "A" into the "F" culture

---

According to the FSMOC model, organizations that have a type "A" culture are predicted to out-perform their competition. Financial measurements that can be used to test this assumption include earnings per share, sales volume, return on equity, stock price, operational costs, and net profit. As for policy recommendations, the FSMOC model suggests that administrative personnel should continue with their current practices.

Organizations that have a type "B" culture are predicted to be financially competitive with other organizations within the same industry. The policy recommendation for these organizations is to incorporate within their organizational culture the missing organizational culture "A" element, and thus form a type "A" culture.

Organizations that have a type "D" culture are predicted to perform below their competitors. The policy recommendation for these organizations is to develop a type "B" or "A" organizational culture.

Organizations that have a type "F" culture are predicted to perform significantly below their competitors. The policy recommendation for these organizations is to incorporate the missing elements of organizational cultures "D," "B," and "A."

The FSMOC Model and the "People Factor"

Organizational cultures A, B, D, and F provide a framework for understanding organizational performance—a framework built on three critical workplace parameters: managerial attitudes and practices in the workplace; the organizational environment among the employees; and the tasks being performed within an organization. At the core of the FSMOC lies a common thread that binds each of the three critical workplace parameters together. This common thread is the driving force that ultimately determines whether or not an organization will possess an A, B, D, or F organizational culture, so it has a fundamental influence on the level of success an organization can achieve. So what is this common thread? The "people" element is the most important factor in any organization. The quality and attitudes of the people within an organization set the stage for its accomplishments. An organization that invests in its employees achieves success in the marketplace. This investment in human capital must begin with the hiring process and continue throughout the employee's tenure with the company. A continual investment in human capital means providing a comprehensive and equitable employment package that, at the minimum, consists of a reasonable pay scale, benefits, and training.

Former U.S. Secretary of Labor Robert Reich strongly believes that when businesses put money into improving the skills of their workers, the investments pay off in increased productivity and improved quality of life for the workers. In his 2002 book *I'll Be Short,* he cited these examples: Granite Rock, a construction materials supplier in Watsonville, California, invests more than $2,000 per employee annually in training—nearly thirteen times the industry average. Workers at Cin-Made, an Ohio firm that makes specialized packaging, receive extensive on-the-job training and additional pay for acquiring advanced skills. And Harley-Davidson, maker of the legendary motorcycles, has established an on-site learning center for its employees. To understand organizational performance, one must understand the "people factor" within an organization. The quality of an organization's people, at all levels, determines organizational success or failure because an organization is nothing more than the system(s) that the members of the organization created, and the superiority of any creation ultimately depends on the abilities of its creator(s). Thus, at the core of organizational performance is the quality of the members of an organization. Failing to recognize this truism leaves the organization in peril.

In summary, what we've discovered so far is that a type "A" organizational culture and putting employees first are two fundamental building blocks of a great place to work. However, just as important and intertwined deep within a type "A" organizational culture and the commitment to putting employees first are the following organizational and managerial principles: (a) the right action principle, (b) social exchange theory, (c) efficiency wages, (d) the eight major categories of a quality of work life (QWL), and (e) the notion of common career anchors.

An organization that truly puts employees first is built upon the right action principle meaning that pursuing organizational goals and objectives should be conducted in such a manner that growth and integrity of people are respected (Johnston cited by Seyfarth, 2005).

A real commitment to employees and the organizational payoffs that flow from that commitment are explained by the social exchange theory, which posits that individuals form relationships with those who can provide valued resources (Umbach, 2007). As mentioned in chapter 7, Umbach further stated:

> In exchange for these resources, individuals will reciprocate (Gouldner, 1960) by providing resources and support. Thus, individuals will exhibit greater commitment to an organization when they feel supported and rewarded (Rhoades, Eisenberger, & Armeli, 2001). This commitment, in turn,

manifests itself in increased performance and other work behaviors that benefit the organization.

Organizations that believe in their employees support them financially by providing an income suitable for maintaining a quality standard of living. Providing a wage higher than that which would equate quantity demanded and quantity supplied is justified by the economic concept known as an efficiency wage—an extra amount paid to employees to encourage them to be more efficient or productive. As employee productivity increases an organization's total costs are reduced; more output can be produced with less workers. In addition, since employees are being paid a higher wage they are less likely to search for a new job resulting in a decrease in turnover and trainings costs.

Crafting an effective organizational culture (a type "A" culture), with the right action principle serving as the foundation and fairly compensating employees for their labor lies at the heart of a great place to work. However, the ultimate macro building blocks of a great place to work are framed within the concepts of a workers' quality of life (QWL) and career anchors. These two concepts encapsulate and expand upon the previous building blocks of a great place to work.

A worker's quality of life can be analyzed according to the following eight factors. The first, an adequate and fair compensation can easily be supported by the economic notion of an efficiency wage. The remaining factors include: a safe and healthy workplace, jobs that develop human capacities, a chance for personal growth and security, a social environment that provides personal identity, freedom from prejudice, a sense of community, and upward mobility, constitutionalism (the rights of personal privacy, dissent, and due process), a work role that minimizes infringement on personal leisure and family needs, and socially responsible organizational actions.

Finally, a great place to work is influenced by the nature of the job tasks and how individuals are allowed to accomplish the task. The most critical characteristics or career anchors associated with a job include: (a) autonomy, (b) influence or control, (c) interesting work, (d) variety, (e) personal/professional growth, (f) working conditions, (g) affiliation, (h) helping people, (i) security, (j) tangible rewards, (k) clearly defined structure and chain of command, (l) recognition as well as (m) challenging goals. Each of the career anchors once again reinforces the notion of creating a workplace that revolves around the employees and the work that they perform.

The bottom line is that organizational decision-makers who want to maximize organizational performance must build their organization upon the building blocks of a great place to work. Only in a great place to work do employees consistently put forth the maximum effort to satisfy customers and achieve organizational greatness. Thus creating a great place to work is the third definitive key to organizational sustainability and success.

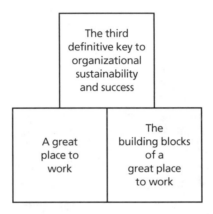

The Critical Points in the Chapter that Lead to the Discovery of the Five Definitive Keys to Organizational Success and Sustainability

Critical Point 1

The building blocks of a great to place are like a large, multicolored patchwork quilt consisting of the following concepts: a type "A" organizational culture, putting employees first, the right action principle, social exchange theory, efficiency wages, quality of work life, and career anchors.

Critical Point 2

Only in a great place to work do employees consistently put the forth the maximum work effort

Critical Point 3

Creating a great place to work is the third definitive key to organizational sustainability and success.

References

Bateman, T. S., & Zeithaml, C. P. (1990). *Management: Function and strategy.* Homewood, IL: Irwin, pp. 538–541

Blau, P. M. (1964). *Exchange and power in social life.* New York: Wiley.

Byham, W. C., & Cox, J. (1988) *Zapp! The lightening of empowerment.* New York: Fawett Columbine Book.

Crosby, P. B. (1986). *Running things: The art of making things happen.* New York: Mentor.

Gouldner, A. W. (1960). The norm of reciprocity: A preliminary statement. *American Sociological Review, 25,* 161–177.

Gwartney, J. D., Stroup, R. L., Sobel, R. S., & Macpherson, D. A. (2009). *Economics: Private and public choice* (12th ed.). Mason, OH: South-Western/ Cengage Learning.

Johnston, B. (1994). Educational administration in the postmodern age. In S. Maxcy, (Ed.), *Postmodern school leadership: Meeting the crisis in educational administration* (pp. 115–131). Westport, CT: Praeger.

Levering, R. (1988). *A great place to work: What makes some employers so good (and most so bad).* New York: Avon Books.

Reich, R. (1983). *The next American frontier.* New York: Penguin Books.

Reich, R. (2002). *I'll be short: Essentials for a decent working society.* Boston: Beacon Press.

Rhoades, L., Eisenberger, R., & Armeli, S. (2001). Affective commitment to an organization: The contribution of perceived organizational support. *Journal of Applied Psychology, 86,* 825–836.

Seyfarth, J. T. (2005). *Human resources management for effective schools* (4th ed.). Boston, MA: Pearson/Allyn and Bacon.

Taylor, J. B. (2007). *Economics* (5th ed.). Boston, MA: Houghton Mifflin Company.

Umbach, P. D. (Winter 2007). How effective are they? Exploring the impact of contingent faculty on undergraduate education, *The Review of Higher Education, 30*(2), 91–123.

PART **4**

Lurking Outside

13

The Cultural Climate of a Nation or Society

The culture of some countries (or regions) is supportive of the capitalist mode of production and lowers the costs of doing business there. Cultural factors can help firms based in such countries achieve a competitive advantage in the world economy.

—Charles W. L. Hill (2000)

Primarily in Western cultures meeting the exact dates of a schedule and a deep sense of urgency in getting tasks accomplished is what drives business. Time is money and work must take priority over family while most Eastern cultures foster a laid-back business philosophy that places family obligations and responsibilities ahead of any business project or schedule. Still other cultures fall somewhere between these two extremes all of which underscores a fundamental truth regarding international business—cultural attitudes regarding business impacts business performance.

Organizational Performance in a Nutshell, pages 85–93
Copyright © 2009 by Information Age Publishing
All rights of reproduction in any form reserved.

Given the importance of culture, what is it? As defined by Edward Tylor (1871), culture is that complex whole which includes knowledge, belief, art, morals, law, custom, and other capabilities acquired by man as a member of society. Geert Hofstede suggested that culture is the collective programming of the mind that distinguishes the members of one human group from another ... Culture, in this sense, includes systems of values. A more succinct definition was offered by Zvi Namenwirth and Robert Weber (1987); culture is a "design for living." Culture is a mixture of elements (social structure, language, education, religion, political and economic philosophy) that exist side by side and as a whole leave an imprint on the behavior of every individual living with-in that culture. In other words, culture acts as the societal glue that binds everyone together.

In today's competitive global marketplace where on the international stage an organization wishes to conduct business is a critical strategic decision that can foster organizational sustainability or inflict a fatal financial wound eventually leading to organizational extinction. To increase the probability of organizational sustainability and reduce the chances of organizational extinction the attributes of a nation that have a substantial impact upon competitiveness must be thoroughly and rationally assessed.

Porter's *Diamond* offers organizational decision-makers a tool for evaluating the economic attractiveness of a nation. According to Porter, four broad attributes (firm strategy, structure, and rivalry; demand conditions; related and supporting industries; and factor endowments) mold the economic environment in which organizations compete:

Firm strategy, structure, and rivalry focuses upon how organizations are created, organized, managed, and the nature of the local rivalry

Demand conditions relates to the demand for the product or service

Related and supporting industries that are available to assist in the production of an organization's product or service

Factor endowments are centered upon the factors of production (land, labor, capital) and the infrastructure

By analyzing these variables (as well as the governmental structure and policies of a nation) an organization can determine the potential benefit of conducting business with-in a nation.

Another evaluation tool is a matrix developed by the International Hough Company which was cited by Philip Kotler (1997) in his book, *Marketing Management: Analysis, Planning, Implementation, and Control.*

According to this matrix, a nation's economic attractiveness can be gauged according to three variables: market attractiveness, risk, and competitive advantage.

Market attractiveness is determined by such factors as GDP, GDP per capita, population growth, skills and availability of the workforce, income distribution, infrastructure, and other economic variables

Risk involves evaluating political, economic, and currency stability as well as repatriation rules.

Competitive advantage deals with such indicators as prior business dealings, whether senior management can work comfortably in a nation, and whether a competitive advantage can be gained

Each of the matrix variables are rated either as low, medium, or high. A nation that has low risk, and high market attractiveness and competitive advantage offers the best probability for achieving organizational success and sustainability.

Once senior management has decided to conduct business operations within a nation then for those organizations that elect to utilize expatriates, as part of their global staffing strategy, it's essential that cross-cultural training (CCT) be provided. A failed expatriate assignment can impose severe explicit costs on an organization as well as implicit costs such as the loss of time and potential business opportunities. Despite the costs of a failed expatriate assignment the evidence tends to indicate that most of the problems that were identified in the 1980s associated with failed expatriate assignments are still with us today (Varner & Palmer, 2002) and thus the development of a well-designed CCT program can be the decisive factor in determining not only expatriate performance but also the over-all international success of an organization. However, it must also be realized that every organization has limited resources to allocate towards employee training. The need for employee training versus the limited organizational resources available for training creates the fundamental training dilemma (Finch, 1989; Wentland, 2003). Overcoming the fundamental training dilemma holds the key to unlocking an organization's ability to compete on the world stage. In this portion of the chapter, the Usable Content Model (UCM) for Expatriate Training is developed. The significance of the model is that it provides organizational decision-makers with a managerial tool for developing a successful CCT program while recognizing the limited resources that an organization can devote towards employee training.

The Fundamental Training Dilemma: Striking a Balance Between Providing Quality Employee Training and Limited Organizational Resources

When establishing any kind of training program it is important to determine the potential content. However, because of corporate constraints, the potential content normally does not comprise the usable content. In other words, the usable content tends to be less than the potential content because of constraints. These constraints include: time, personnel and budgetary limitations, facilities, and the attitude of senior management towards training. The relationship between potential and usable content can be expressed as:

The Content Decision-Making Formula

Usable Content = Potential Content – Constraints
(Finch, 1989)

Thus any training program must balance the need to provide employees with the proper level of training weighted against corporate constraints. A tilt one-way or the other could have detrimental repercussions upon the organization. Too much training is an unnecessary waste of corporate resources. Too little training could result in an organization being unable to achieve a competitive advantage in the marketplace. In terms of a (CCT) program the failure to maintain the delicate balance between training content set against a backdrop of organizational constraints can directly result in both the failure of an expatriate assignment as well as the international strategic goals of the corporation. Expatriate failure can be defined as the premature return of an expatriate manager to his or her home country or an expatriate who remains on his (or her) assignment for the entire duration but is considered ineffective (Dowling, Welch, & Schuler, 1999; Hill, 2000; Edmond, 2002). Current research tends to suggest that between 25 to 40 percent of American expatriates posted to developed countries return early. That number increases to 70 percent for expatriates working in developing countries. Research has also indicated that the cost of failed expatriate assignments can range from $250,000 to $1 million (Vermond, 2001; Varner & Palmer, 2002; Jones, 2002). In addition, approximately 30 to 50 percent of American expatriates who stay at their international assignments are considered ineffective or marginally effective by their firms (Hill, 2000).

A Suggestion for Reducing Expatriate Failure Rates

Many of the factors associated with failed expatriate assignments (lack of or inadequate selection criteria, cross-cultural training, compensation, repatriation and other human resource policies including career blockage and employee disciplinary as well as "general" culture shock issues and the inability of spouse to adjust to the foreign assignment) can be reduced by utilizing the Usable Content Model for Expatriate Training. In sum, an international organization can reduce its expatriate failure rate by improving the expatriate selection process and establishing an effective CCT program:

The purpose of the selection process is to determine the compatibility and receptiveness of an employee and his (or her) family to an assignment overseas. A thorough selection process must also be capable of developing a pool of qualified candidates for international management positions. Ingo Theuerkauf developed a model, which illustrates the stages of a thorough selection process. The stages in the model include: recruiting worldwide, applying company-wide screening for international talent, creating opportunities to gain substantial international experience, and finally, promoting to senior management positions (Czinkota, 1996).

An effective CCT program can foster an understanding of the host country's culture, history, and heritage so that the expatriate can function accordingly. CCT can also provide the newly assigned expatriate with some understanding of the ways of doing business in the country of assignment that can be very different from the ways of doing business in the home country (Ashamalla, 1997). The alternative to not providing an effective CCT program is the increased possibility of a failed expatriate assignment and the potential loss of business opportunities, damaged relations with the firm's constituencies in the host country as well as a long-term negative impact upon the firm's reputation in the region (Ashamalla, 1997). To avoid such costs, senior management should provide an expatriate with CCT and a model that can be utilized to determine the structure of an effective CCT program is the Usable Content Model.

The Usable Content Model for Expatriate Training

Length of assignment	Special project	Fill a position within the organizational hierarchy
Less than six months	**Familiarization Training Approach** Length of training (3 to 4 days)	**Harmonization Training Approach** Length of training (5 to 7 days)
Greater than six months	**Unification Training Approach** Length of training (3 to 5 weeks)	

The Usable Content Model is built upon the premise that the length and content of an effective CCT program depends on the length and the type of expatriate assignment. The UCM also recognizes that corporate constraints tend to reduce both the course content and length of training provided to employees. Therefore, the UCM takes into account both potential and usable content. Potential content is referred to as the Unification Training Approach (UTA). Usable content is referred to as the Familiarization Training Approach (FTA) and the Harmonization Training Approach (HTA). The FTA includes providing area briefings, cultural briefings, films/ books about the host country, and cultural sensitivity training. The length of the FTA is between three to four days. The HTA includes the content of the FTA plus role-playing, critical incidents and case studies. The length of the HTA is between five to seven days. The UTA includes the content of the two previous training approaches plus complete CCT for the employee's family and an overseas trip to the host country. An overseas trip allows the employee and his (or her) family to obtain "firsthand" experience in their new environment. The length of the UTA is between three to five weeks.

The Conclusions of the Usable Content Model for Expatriate Training

The UCM illustrates that if the length of an expatriate assignment is less than six months and the nature of the assignment is a special project then the effective CCT program should be the Familiarization Training Approach. If the length of an expatriate assignment is less than six months and the nature of the assignment is to fill an organizational position within the corporate hierarchy then the effective CCT program should be the Harmonization Training Approach. If the length of an expatriate assignment is greater than six months then the effective CCT program should be the

Unification Training Approach. As for any language training, the following guide is recommended.

Length of assignment	Host country's primary language is different from home country's primary language		The expatriate can already communicate (oral & written) in the host country's language	
	Yes	No	Yes	No
Less than six months	Survival language training and use of interpreters	No training is necessary	No training is necessary	Survival language training and use of interpreters
Greater than six months	Extensive language training	No training is necessary	No training is necessary	Extensive language training

The Usable Content Model provides firms with a specific managerial tool for overcoming the problem of expatriate failure rates and thus eliminates a critical obstacle that stands in the way of achieving global strategic objectives.

A Final Chapter Comment

Firms operating a business in a foreign country face many problems. However, by carefully analyzing the culture with in a nation and providing CCT the chances of obtaining consistent profitability is greatly enhanced; and this realization opens the door to the fourth definitive key of organizational success and sustainability. In short, organizational decision-makers must understand the culture in which their organization operates.

The Critical Points in the Chapter that Lead to the Discovery of the Five Definitive Keys to Organizational Success and Sustainability

Critical Point 1

The culture of a nation impacts the chances of organizational success and sustainability.

Critical Point 2

Two models to evaluate the critical attributes of a nation are Porter's Diamond and the International Hough Company Matrix.

Critical Point 3

For organizations that elect to utilize expatriates, the Usable Content Model can serve as a guide for reducing expatriate failure rates.

Critical Point 4

By carefully analyzing the culture with in a nation and providing CCT the chances of obtaining consistent profitability is greatly enhanced; and this realization opens the door to the fourth definitive key of organizational success and sustainability. In short, organizational decision-makers must understand the culture in which their organization operates.

References

Ashamalla, M., & Crocitto, M. (1997). Easing entry and beyond: Preparing expatriates and patriates for foreign assignment success. *International Journal of Commerce and Management, 7*(2).

Black, S. (Winter 1989). A practical but theory-based framework for selecting cross-cultural training methods, *HR Management, 4*(28).

Brewster, C., & Pickard, J. (Fall 1994). Evaluating expatriate training. *International Studies of Management and Organization, 3*(24).

Czinkota, M., Ronkainen, I. A., & Moffett, M. H. (1996). *International business.* Orlando, FL: The Dryden Press.

Dowling, P., Welch, D. E., & Schuler, R. S. (1999). *International human resource management* (3rd ed.). Mason. OH: South-Western College.

Edmond, S. (Fall 2002). Exploring the success of expatriates of U.S. multinational firms in Mexico. *International Trade Journal, 3*(16).

Finch, C. & Crunkilton, J. (1989). *Curriculum development in vocational and technical education: Planning, content, and implementation.* Boston, MA: Allyn and Bacon, 1989.

Harvey, M. (Winter 1996). The Selection of Managers for Foreign Assignments. *Columbia Journal of World Business, 4*(31).

Hill, C. (2000). *International business: Competing in the global marketplace.* New York: Irwin-McGraw-Hill, pp. 79, 139.

Hofstede, G. (Fall 1983). The cultural relativity of organizational practices and theories. *Journal of International Business Studies,* 75–89.

Hofstede, G. (1984). *Culture's consequences: International differences in work related values.* Beverly Hills, CA: Sage, p. 21.

Jones, H. (September 15, 2002). Cost pressures cause corporations to rethink their expatriate approach. *Wall Street Journal,* p. D5.

Katz, J., & Seifer, D. (1996). It's a different world out there: planning for expatriate success through selection, pre-departure training and on-site socialization. *Human Resources Planning, 2*(19).

Kotler, P. (1997). *Marketing management: Analysis, planning, implementation, and control* (9th ed.). Upper Saddle River, NJ: Prentice Hall, pp. 408–409.

Mendenhall, M., Dunbar, E., & Oddou, G. (Fall 1987). Expatriate selection, training and career pathing: A review and critique. *Human Resources Management, 3*(26).

Namenwirth, J. Z., & Weber, R. B. (1987). *Dynamics of culture.* Boston, MA: Allen & Unwin, p. 8.

Porter, M. E. (1990). *The competitive advantage of nations.* New York: Free Press

Shumsky, N. (Sept/Oct 2002). Justifying the intercultural training investment. *Journal of European Business, 1*(4).

Tylor, E. B. (1871). *Primitive culture.* London: Murray.

Varner, I., & Palmer, T. (Spring 2002). Successful expatriation and organizational strategies. *Review of Business, 2*(23).

Vermond, K. (October 2001). Expatriates come home. *CMA Management 7*(75).

Wentland, D. (May/June 2003). A new practical guide for determining expatriate compensation: The comprehensive model. *Compensation and Benefits Review, 3*(35).

Wentland, D. (Winter 2003). The strategic training of employees model: Balancing organizational constraints and training content. *The Advanced Management Journal, 1*(68).

14

Competitors (Industry and Firms) and the Chance Factor

One of the characteristics of a free market system is that suppliers have the right to compete with one another.

—Gitman & McDaniel (2003, p. 31)

According to economists there are four product markets in which goods and services are brought and sold. The markets have been identified as: (a) perfect competition, (b) a monopoly, (c) monopolistic competition, and (d) an oligopoly. What primarily distinguishes one market from another is the notion of market structure meaning the number of producers (suppliers). In a perfectly competitive market there are many producers selling similar products while in a monopoly only one producer supplies the product. Sandwiched between perfect competition and a monopoly are monopolistic competition, many producers selling differentiated products; and an oligopoly where only a few producers manufacture most or all of the output.

Organizational Performance in a Nutshell, pages 95–107

In terms of market structure, what's most important for consumers is the number of producers because competition among many suppliers forces each organization to focus upon productivity and develop strategic plans to achieve a competitive advantage. An understanding of the strategic planning process will provide a framework for analyzing why an organization exists and how it continues to survive against competing entities.

The business landscape is littered with examples of companies that have failed to maximize stakeholder value because they lost their direction or drifted into all sorts of business ventures without first acquiring the knowledge and expertise to manage those ventures. A classic example is Sears, which in 1981 expanded into real estate and financial services, only to experience a decline in its core business of retailing. By 1993, Sears had sold all its financial units, yet it continued to experience sales and image problems in its retailing division. Sears still has not recovered from its management team's misadventure into uncharted waters (where Sears had limited or no experience). The company's series of missteps culminated when Kmart took over Sears in November of 2004. The once-powerful number-one retailer in the nation was reduced to the status of take-over victim, and is now playing a secondary role to another struggling retail company. The lesson to be learned is that poor managerial decisions can cause a company to lose its identity, resulting in an overall lack of direction and purpose that eventually diverts and dilutes the human resource capabilities of an organization. Sears was a major retailer, but when it lost its focus on retail, its financial performance eroded.

The role of strategic planning is to keep an organization on track and focused on the activities that it does best so that it does not drift into mediocrity. Strategic planning should improve management decision-making and give the company a competitive advantage or allow it to remain competitive in the marketplace. The hallmarks of strategic planning are analysis, development of a course of action aimed at achieving a competitive advantage, implementation of that course of action, constant feedback, and taking corrective measures when necessary. The holy grail of the strategic planning process is to learn how to make better managerial decisions, as measured by the competitive advantage that the organization achieves over its rivals.

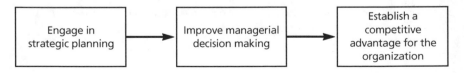

The Strategic Planning Process

In 1980, Derek F. Abell (1980) proposed that the framework of the strategic planning process could be built on the answers to three critical questions:

- Who is being satisfied?
- What is being satisfied?
- How are the needs of the customers being satisfied?

If you determine who is being satisfied, you can identify the customer base (or target market). The other two questions focus attention on the needs of the target market, and how an organization can best meet those needs. In essence, the three questions proposed by Abell form the basis by which organizational decision makers identify or define the purpose of the organization.

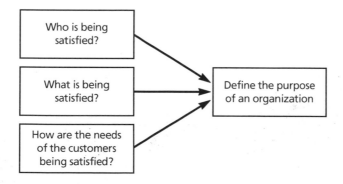

Thus, the strategic planning process is utilized to systematically address the questions proposed by Abell (1980); it is also the phase during which managers choose a set of strategies. The strategic planning process consists of five basic steps that can be followed simultaneously.

Step 1 Formulate the corporate mission and vision statements, and identify the major organizational goals.

Step 2 Analyze the organization's external competitive environment to identify opportunities and threats.

Step 3 Analyze the organization's internal operating environment to identify the organization's strengths and weaknesses.

Step 4   Select strategies that build on the organization's strengths and correct its weaknesses, to take advantage of external opportunities and counter external threats.

Step 5   Implement strategy. Design appropriate organizational structures and control systems to put the organization's chosen strategy into action.

If we look at strategic planning from a different angle, we see that the process can be separated into two dimensions: strategy and operational effectiveness. Michael Porter, a business professor at Harvard University (and probably the leading authority on strategic planning) believes that *strategy* is a plan for competing in the marketplace, whereas *operational effectiveness* is the ability to perform operational tasks more efficiently than do competitors. The end product of the strategic planning process for an organization should be to establish a competitive advantage over its rivals.

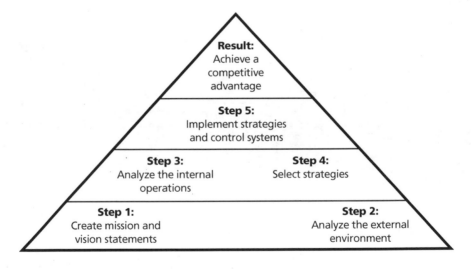

Competitive Advantage

Some experts contend that competitive advantage is really a strategy to give an organization a distinct advantage over its competition. According to Michael Porter in his 1985 work *Competitive Advantage,* an organization must select a competitive strategy in order to successfully perform at an above-average profitability level because no firm can be all things to all people. Porter proposed three competitive strategy options: cost leadership, a differentiation strategy, and a focus strategy.

Cost leadership is a strategy in which an organization attempts to be the lowest-cost producer in its industry. A firm can obtain a low-cost advantage through efficient operations, economies of scale, technological innovation, low-cost labor, or preferential access to raw materials.

A *differentiation* strategy occurs when an organization attempts to distinguish itself from its industry competitors within a broad market. To achieve a differentiation strategy, an organization strives to obtain a unique position in the marketplace by emphasizing high quality, extraordinary service, an innovative product design, technological capability, or an unusually positive brand image. The key is that the unique position that the company is attempting to establish must be significantly different from its rivals to justify a price premium that exceeds the cost of differentiating.

A *focus* strategy is when an organization wants to establish an advantage in a narrow market segment. The focus strategy utilizes either a cost advantage or a differentiation approach aimed at a narrow market segment.

In order to achieve long-term success, an organization must sustain its competitive advantage. Tactics that organizations use to achieve a long-run competitive advantage include establishing barriers to entry, such as patents, copyrights, trademarks, or economies of scale. Firms sometimes lower prices to gain market share, tie up suppliers with exclusive contracts, or lobby Congress to impose trade restrictions designed to limit foreign competition.

Underlying Porter's three competitive strategies are the generic building blocks of competitive advantage, as described by Charles W. L. Hill and Gareth R. Jones (1998):

1. Superior efficiency is about converting inputs into outputs. Inputs are the basic factors of production, such as labor, land, capital, management, and technological know-how. Outputs are the goods and services that an organization produces. The more efficiently an organization can convert inputs into outputs, the higher the productivity level of that organization. The organization with the highest level of productivity in an industry typically has the lowest costs of production, and therefore gains a competitive advantage.

2. The impact of superior product quality on competitive advantage is twofold. First, providing high-quality products increases the value of those products in the eyes of the consumer (target market) that allows the firm to charge a higher price. The second impact of high quality on competitive advantage comes from the greater efficiency and lower unit cost it brings.

3. Superior innovation is the most important of the building blocks of competitive advantage. Innovation can be defined as anything new or novel about the way a company operates or about the products it produces. Innovative organizations provide consumers with products that are not available from other firms. That lack of availability allows the organization to charge a premium for its product. In addition, innovative organizations can build brand loyalty, which makes it more difficult for rivals to gain market share.

4. Superior customer service or responsiveness is achieved by identifying and satisfying the needs of the consumers (target market) better than any other organization. Superior customer responsiveness includes such activities as quality, customization, response time, design, and superior service before and after the sale.

Organizations that focus on the building blocks of competitive advantage increase the probability of improving the firm's bottom line. When everything else is all said and done, increasing the bottom line *is* the bottom line!

Improving the financial results of the organization

Competitive strategies
- Cost leadership
- Differentiation strategy
- Focus strategy

The building blocks of competitive advantage
- Superior efficiency
- Superior product quality
- Superior innovation
- Superior customer sevice or responsiveness

Output Value Creation and Competitive Advantage

Another important concept connected with the building blocks of competitive advantage is the notion of output value creation—the value of the product or service produced by an organization. An organization creates output value by developing a strategic plan that focuses on the building blocks of competitive advantage. This plan should address the needs of the target market and the employees. In this context, the target market will be specifically referred to as a group of people for which an organization designs, implements, and maintains a strategic plan intended to meet the needs of that group, resulting in mutually satisfying exchanges. The output value generated by an organization is measured by the equation $V = B/P$ (the letter V represents value; B represents perceived and/or actual benefits; and P represents the price of the product). A higher output value as perceived by the target market increases the probability of gaining market share and improving profitability.

Output Value Creation and Putting Employees First

Lurking beneath the equation ($V = B/P$) is the ability of the workforce and individual employees to create product benefits in an efficient manner. The lesson to be learned is that to enhance the output value-creation process, an organization needs to put its employees first. Here is how Thompson and Stickland (2003) put it:

> Organizations with a spirit of high performance typically are intensely people-oriented, and they reinforce their concern for individual employees on every conceivable occasion in every conceivable way. They treat employees with dignity and respect, train each employee thoroughly, encourage employees to use their own initiative and creativity in performing their work, set reasonable and clear performance standards, hold managers at every level responsible for developing the people who report to them, and grant employees enough autonomy to stand out, excel, and contribute. Creating a results-oriented organizational culture generally entails making champions out of the people who turn in winning performances.

As alluded to in chapters 3 and 11, at its basic level, high performance essentially revolves around knowing how the abilities of each employee differ, and using that knowledge to increase the likelihood that any employee will consistently perform his or her job well. Employee job performance begins the "chain" of workplace activity that determines the level of productivity that a group or organization will eventually achieve. Productive environments at the group or organizational level are linked to and depend on the performance of each employee. Like any link in a chain, the productivity that a group or organization can achieve is only as high as the weakest link in the chain of workplace activity. Group accomplishments and organizational productivity are a function of individual accomplishments and productivity.

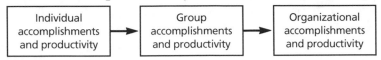

Chain of Workplace Activity that Influences Productivity

(A group refers to a department or major function within an organization.)

Also recall, from chapters 3 and 11, how well an employee performs on the job will be reflective of the employee's intellectual and physical abilities, as well as the job fit between an employee's abilities and the job task. *Intellectual ability* refers to an employee's capability to do mental activities. The seven most frequently cited dimensions making up intellectual abilities are listed below, as explained by Stephen Robbins (2001):

1. *Number aptitude* is the ability to do speedy and accurate arithmetic.
2. *Verbal comprehension* is the ability to understand what is read or heard and the relationship between the words.
3. *Perceptual speed* is the ability to identify visual similarities and differences quickly and accurately.
4. *Inductive reasoning* is the ability to identify a logical sequence in a problem, and then to solve the problem.
5. *Deductive reasoning* is the ability to use logic and assess the implications of an argument.
6. *Spatial visualization* is the ability to imagine how an object would look if its position in space were changed.
7. *Memory* is the ability to retain and recall past experiences.

Physical ability refers to the stamina, dexterity, strength, and similar characteristics that are required to perform a task. The nine basic abilities involved in the performance of physical tasks are listed below, from the same source:

1. *Dynamic strength* is the ability to exert muscular force repeatedly or continuously over time.
2. *Trunk strength* is the ability to exert muscular strength using the trunk (particularly abdominal) muscles.
3. *Static strength* is the ability to exert force against external objects.

4. *Explosive strength* is the ability to expend a maximum of energy in one or a series of explosive acts.
5. *Extent flexibility* is the ability to move the trunk and back muscles as far as possible.
6. *Dynamic flexibility* is the ability to make rapid, repeated flexing movements.
7. *Body coordination* is the ability to coordinate the simultaneous actions of different parts of the body.
8. *Balance* is the ability to maintain equilibrium, despite forces pulling off-balance.
9. *Stamina* is the ability to continue maximum effort when prolonged effort is required over time.

To maximize employee performance, you must match the intellectual and physical abilities of an employee to the job. When the employee ability–job match is out of equilibrium because the employee's abilities exceed or are not sufficient to perform the task, the performance level of the employee will be marginal, at best. Marginally performing employees result in underperforming groups and an unproductive, non-competitive organization.

The Employee Ability–Job Match Is Out of Equilibrium When...

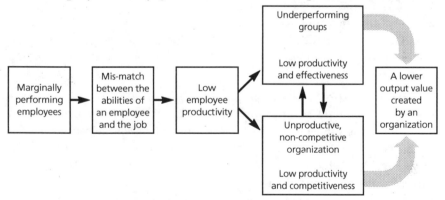

(A group refers to a department or major function within an organization.)

On the other hand, when the employee ability–job match is in equilibrium, an unproductive workplace can be transformed into a productive environment that generates a high output value. This transformation requires that the commitments to put employees first and provide quality training programs be linked to the strategic planning process. An organization that blends these commitments with the strategic planning process creates a work environment dedicated to enhancing the abilities and skills of their employees. Within this type of work environment, employee productivity is nourished and can grow. As employee productivity expands, output value increases.

The Employee Ability–Job Match Is in Equilibrium When . . .

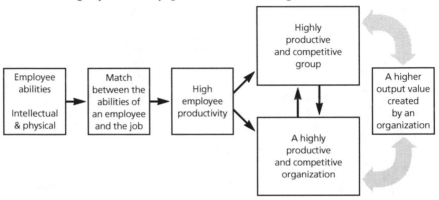

Focusing upon your employees and relating their abilities to the tasks that are required to accomplish the strategic objectives of the organization creates an environment where the output value-creation process can flourish, just as long-overdue rain can transform a barren patch of land into a garden oasis.

How well an organization integrates within the strategic planning process its commitments to put employees first will have a dramatic impact upon the output value created by the organization. Creating output value is what's behind establishing a competitive advantage in the marketplace. Organizations that achieve organizational sustainability must establish a competitive advantage. Thus, the fifth definitive key to organizational success is achieving a competitive advantage in the marketplace.

A Note About the Chance Factor

No matter how well an organization plans there is always the chance that a random, unforeseen, and unpredictable event will occur. These chance events can easily derail or provide a benefit to an organization. The chance factor can explain why an organization might be able to succeed in the marketplace despite itself. The chance factor can also account for the demise of an organization that appeared to have all or most of the definitive keys working to its advantage.

Just like in life, a chance occurrence can dramatically alter an individual's life and that is true for an organization as well, a chance event can have a positive or negative impact that influences organizational success and sustainability. A chance event cannot be planned for, or predicted; it just happens. When a chance event does occur an organization will have no other option other than to pick up the pieces, if it's a negative event. If the chance event happens to be positive then an organization gets to reap the benefits for as long as possible without doing anything. Organization's that have worked hard at obtaining the five definitive keys to organizational success and sustainability have a higher probability of surviving a negative chance event and by the same token will accumulate more benefits from a positive chance event. Thus, even with a chance event, the five definitive keys to organizational success and sustainability have a dramatic influence upon which organizations will thrive and the ones that will become extinct.

Chance events include (but are not limited to) fluctuations in the business cycle, natural disasters, and suddenly changing world events.

The Critical Points in the Chapter that Lead to the Discovery of the Five Definitive Keys to Organizational Success and Sustainability

Critical Point 1

There are four product markets: perfect competition, monopoly, monopolistic competition, and an oligopoly. The number of competitors primarily distinguishes one market from another.

Critical Point 2

An understanding of the strategic planning process will provide a framework for analyzing why an organization exists and how it continues to survive against competing entities.

Critical Point 3

The holy grail of the strategic planning process is to learn how to make better managerial decisions as measured by the competitive advantage that an organization achieves over its rivals.

Critical Point 4

According to Michael Porter an organization can obtain three competitive options: cost leadership, a differentiation strategy, or a focus strategy.

Critical Point 5

Underlying Porter's three competitive strategies are the genetic building blocks of competitive advantage: superior efficiency, superior product quality, superior innovation, and superior customer service or responsiveness.

Organizations that focus on the building blocks of competitive advantage increase the probability of improving the firm's bottom line. Increasing the bottom line is the bottom line!

Critical Point 6

Output value creation stems from the building blocks of competitive advantage.

Critical Point 7

Output value is measured by the equation: $V = B/P$.

Critical Point 8

The skills and abilities of the employees have a critical impact output value.

Critical Point 9

The skills of an employee are determined by the employee's intellectual and physical abilities.

Critical Point 10

Matching an employee's ability to the job increases output value.

Critical Point 11

Ultimately, creating output value is the result of establishing a competitive advantage in the marketplace.

Thus the fifth definitive key to organizational success and sustainability is to achieve a competitive advantage in the marketplace.

Critical Point 12

A chance event can either derail or provide a benefit to an organization and it cannot be planned for, or predicted; chance events just happen.

Critical Point 13

When a chance event occurs, the five definitive keys to organizational success and sustainability have a dramatic influence upon which organizations will thrive and the ones that will become extinct.

Chance events include (but are not limited to) fluctuations in the business cycle, natural disasters, and suddenly changing world events.

References

Abell, D. F. (1980). *Defining the business: The starting point of strategic planning.* Englewood Cliffs, NJ: Prentice Hall.

Gitman, L. J., & McDaniel, C. (2003). *The best of the future of business.* Mason: OH: South-Western.

Hill, C., & Jones, G. R. (1998). *Strategic management: An integrated approach* (4th ed.). Boston: Houghton Mifflin, pp. 4, 6, 45.

Keen, P., & Morton, S. (1978). *Decision support systems: An organizational perspective.* Reading, MA: Addison-Wesley, pp. 61–77.

Merrick, A., & Bermna, D. K. (November 18, 2004). "Kmart to buy Sears for $11.5 billion," *Wall Street Journal,* p. A1

Moorhead, G., & Griffin, R. (1995) *Organizational behavior: Managing people and organization.* Boston: Houghton Mifflin.

Porter, M. (1980). *Competitive strategy: Techniques for analyzing industries and competitors.* New York: The Free Press.

Porter, M. (1985). *Competitive advantage: Creating and sustaining superior performance.* New York: The Free Press.

Robbins, S. (2001). *Organizational behavior* (9th ed.). Upper Saddle River, NJ: Prentice Hall, pp. 37–38.

Sage, A. (September 1981). Behavioral and organizational considerations in the design of information systems and processes for planning and decision support. *IEEE Transactions on Systems, Man, and Cybernetics, SMC-11, 9,* 640–678.

Thompson, A., & Strickland, A. J., III. (2003). *Strategic management: Concepts and cases* (13th ed.). New York: McGraw-Hill/Irwin, pp. 439, 440.

PART 5

Concluding the Voyage:
Organizational Performance in a Nutshell

15

Organizational Survival or Failure

*It is of the highest importance in the art of detection to be able to recognize,
out of a number of facts, which are incidental and which are vital.*
—Sherlock Holmes
(Thomas, 1998, p. 96)

In Larry Millett's (1996) book *Sherlock Holmes and the Red Demon,* Sherlock Holmes is asked the following question:

"Now, Mr. Holmes, what will you need to begin your investigation?"

Holmes replied, "The facts. They are the foundation of all that will follow..."

In management's never-ending quest to improve performance, organizations chase after the most-recent technological breakthroughs or the latest marketing techniques or the "hottest" trends in leadership or finance theory the same way puppies race in circles trying to catch their tails. After

111

all that frantic scrambling around, what tends to emerge from those efforts are short-term cost reductions and momentary spikes in some numbers on quarterly accounting reports—no long-term solutions to organizational competitiveness and success.

Steady, long-term competitiveness requires that organizational decision-makers understand and work towards crafting an organization built around the five definitive keys to organizational success and sustainability. It's the five definitive keys that generate maximum output value. Without a true commitment to the five definitive keys at all levels throughout an organization, the journey to enhance organizational performance will be an elusive adventure.

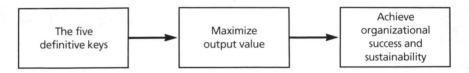

Output maximization requires an organization to provide a better value to consumers than a competitor. As stated by Brimley and Garfield (2008) consumer sovereignty is the willingness to pay for a good and it's the willingness to pay for a good that generates revenues for an organization. Goods or services that fail to satisfy consumers eventually are forced from the marketplace and drain the financial strength from an organization. If left unchecked the organization will eventually cease to exist.

Organizational success and sustainability depends upon satisfying consumers and fulfilling the needs of a consumer is more effectively accomplished by organizations that focus upon the five definitive keys. The virtuous cycle of maximizing output value by providing consumers with the best products available begins and ends with the five definitive keys of organizational success and sustainability. A virtuous circle is a condition in which a favorable circumstance or result gives rise to another that subsequently supports the first; and in terms of organizational success and sustainability it's all about the five definitive keys.

The Virtuous Circle of the Five Definitive Keys of Organizational Success and Sustainability

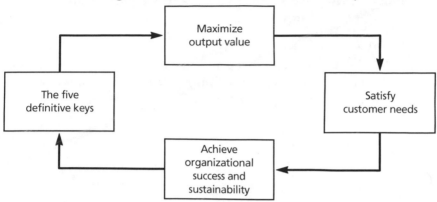

The virtuous circle of the five definitive keys to organizational success and sustainability provides a straightforward picture of our journey that triumphantly ended by unearthing the facts regarding organizational performance.

As a final recap of our voyage, let's utilize the following rating scale.

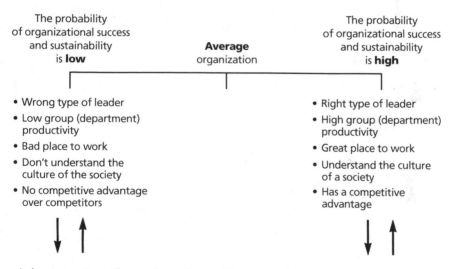

A chance event can tilt an outcome in a positive or negative manner for an organization

That's organizational performance in a nutshell!

The Critical Points in the Chapter that Lead to the Discovery of the Five Definitive Keys to Organizational Success and Sustainability

Critical Point 1

It's the five definitive keys that generate maximum output value. Without a true commitment to the five definitive keys at all levels throughout an organization, the journey to enhance organizational performance will be an elusive adventure.

Critical Point 2

The probability of organizational success and sustainability is low when: (1) wrong type of leader; (2) low group (department) productivity; (3) bad place to work; (4) don't understand the culture of the society; and (5) no competitive advantage over competitors

Critical Point 3

The probability of organizational success and sustainability is high when: (1) right type of leader; (2) high group (department) productivity; (3) great place to work; (4) understand the culture of the society; and (5) has a competitive advantage over competitors

Critical Point 4

A chance event can tilt an outcome in a positive or negative manner for an organization

References

Brimley, V. Jr., & Garfield, R. R. (2008). *Financing education in a climate of change* (10th ed.). Boston: Pearson.

Millett, L. (1996). *Sherlock Holmes and the Red Demon.* New York: Viking.

Thomas, D. (1998). *The secret cases of Sherlock Holmes.* New York: Carroll & Graf.

16

The Future

. . . there are laws that govern chaos just as there are laws that govern
the rest of the natural world. I know that sounds contradictory,
but there is order to disorder.

—James David (2006, p. 45)

The global economic environment will continue to force organizations to confront competitors from any where on the planet. The demand and supply forces of the marketplace insure that only the most innovative and financially strong firms will survive, the weak will become extinct. As organizational success and sustainability becomes more precarious the men and women in charge of managing organizations must focus upon the five definitive keys. For those organizations not centered upon the five definitive keys the likelihood of organizational failure is greatly increased.

Let's recap the five definitive keys of organizational success and sustainability:

The First Definitive Key to Organizational Success and Sustainability

Fill organizational leadership positions with the right type of leaders— meaning individuals who possess the "right type of leader" characteristics

Organizational Performance in a Nutshell, pages 115–117
Copyright © 2009 by Information Age Publishing
All rights of reproduction in any form reserved.

described in chapter 10. CREEPS must be eliminated from any leadership or managerial position.

The Second Definitive Key to Organizational Success and Sustainability

Understand how to maximize group/department performance as outlined in chapter 11 or organizational performance will not be maximized

The Third Definitive Key to Organizational Success and Sustainability

Create a great place to work as described in chapter 12 where employees will want to exert the maximum effort, not the minimum effort.

The Fourth Definitive Key to Organizational Success and Sustainability

By carefully analyzing the culture with-in a nation and providing cross-cultural training (CCT) the chances of obtaining consistent profitability is greatly enhanced. In short, organizational decision-makers must understand the culture in which their organization operates.

The Fifth Definitive Key to Organizational Success and Sustainability

Obtain a competitive advantage over competitors in the marketplace as summarized in chapter 14.

The Chance Factor

As mentioned in chapter 14, a chance factor can dramatically alter an organization. Organization's that are built around the five definitive keys to organizational success and sustainability have a higher probability of surviving a negative chance event and by the same token will accumulate more benefits from a positive chance event.

The illustration below provides a final way to summarize organizational survivability.

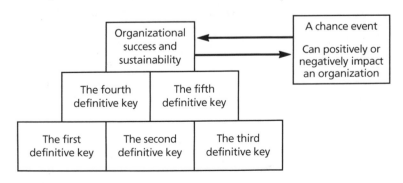

Ignoring the five definitive keys to organizational success and sustainability will jeopardize organizational survivability. The five definitive keys are the laws that guide organizational performance.

As stated by Steve Berry (2007) ... "the measure of an idea was how relative it was not only to its time, but beyond" (p. 120). The five definitive keys to organizational success and sustainability summarize organizational performance in a nutshell; now and in the future.

The Critical Points in the Chapter that Lead to the Discovery of the Five Definitive Keys to Organizational Success and Sustainability

Critical Point 1

The five definitive keys are the principles that govern organizational performance now and in the future and as such summarize organizational performance in a nutshell.

Critical Point 2

Ignore the five definitive keys and jeopardize your organization's ability to achieve organizational success and sustainability

References

Berry, S. (2007). *The Alexandria link.* New York: Ballantine Books.

David, J. (2006). *Thunder of time.* New York: Forge Books/Tom Doherty, LLC.

Appendix

Summary of Critical Points

For those pressed for time, the critical points of each chapter have been summarized on the following pages. Like any short cut it efficiently gets you to your destination, but many of the most interesting and rewarding sights of the trip tend to get missed in your hurry to get from point A to B.

Combining the summary points with a full reading of each chapter will provide a comprehensive understanding of the five definitive keys to organizational success and sustainability.

Chapter 1

Critical Point 1

To maximize output an organization needs to put employees first. Many organizations claim to put their employees first; few do.

Critical Point 2

As important as the commitment to the employees is, that concept represents just a glimpse into organizational performance. Ultimately, organizational performance depends upon understanding the five definitive keys to organizational success and sustainability.

Organizational Performance in a Nutshell, pages 119–128
Copyright © 2009 by Information Age Publishing

Chapter 2

Critical Point 1

The management-employee relationship paradigm needs to become more of a partnership rather than being viewed as an arrangement in which one group is subordinate to the other.

Critical Point 2

Organizations that adopt the new management-employee relationship and demonstrate a clear concern for their employees will create a workplace in which employees are more likely to put forth a maximum effort; not a minimum.

Critical Point 3

Understanding organizational performance begins with understanding ourselves and the right kind of leader that is required to sustain organizational effectiveness and efficiency.

Chapter 3

Critical Point 1

Unmasking ourselves forms the foundation upon which individual, group, and organizational performance can thrive or wither. Understanding ourselves and how we influence the workplace is the first leg of our journey towards discovering the five definitive key of organizational success.

Critical Point 2

Only through an examination of the self can we begin the process of understanding the right type of leader, meaning a leader who wants to change the traditional management-employee paradigm to the new management-employee relationship that was outlined in chapter 2.

Chapter 4

Critical Point 1

Perception influences our behavior and actions and thus provides a glimpse into unmasking who we really are.

Critical Point 2

The *Four Casual Factors of Success or Failure* can be utilized to realistically analyze a situation and diagnose our behavior and actions. Ultimately, this diagnosis allows us to continue our voyage towards discovering what lies at the core of our being.

Chapter 5

Critical Point 1

The Personality characteristics of the right type of leader include: an individual who can easily adapt to various situations, is sociable, conscientious, tactful, considerate, and open to various points of view.

Chapter 6

Critical Point 1

The combination of culture and life experiences such as our family environment, the location(s) where we grew up, the schools we attended, the work situations we encountered, our love relationships and the friends we have chosen are probably responsible for approximately 50% of our personality.

Critical Point 2

The right type of leader is not interested in him or her self but instead is focused upon the conditions of all those individuals who work for them. By truly caring about the employees, the right type of leader will achieve unparalleled organizational success.

Chapter 7

Critical Point 1

Employees with a high level of job satisfaction and job involvement tend to also have a high regard for the organization.

Critical Point 2

A high level of job satisfaction, job involvement, and organizational commitment stems from matching the physical and intellectual abilities of an employee with the job.

Critical Point 3

The Job Characteristics Model (JCM) can be utilized to understand the dimensions of a job.

Critical Point 4

When employees are well suited for the job remarkable gains in productivity can be achieved and make no mistake about it, productivity is the key to economic and organizational success.

Critical Point 5

Productive employees are motivated employees. Motivation is the willingness of an individual to exert high levels of effort. Employees are willing and able to exert a high level of effort when the employee ability–job match is in equilibrium, when recognition is provided for accomplishments and when opportunities for advancement are available for those employees who desire that.

Critical Point 6

Social exchange theory posits that individuals will exhibit greater commitment to an organization when they feel supported and rewarded.

Critical Point 7

Making a "true" commitment to the employees is what separates the right type of leader from the rest and it's that commitment that inspires the employees to want to accomplish organizational goals in the most efficient and effective manner. In other words, the right type of leader can motivate and lead others towards achieving extraordinary organizational results.

Chapter 8

Critical Point 1

A journey of self-discovery means risking a peek at something we may not want to see; but in the final analysis life is all about seeing, learning and growing.

Chapter 9

Critical Point 1

Barriers to change include: selective information processing, fear of the unknown, habit, and security.

Critical Point 2

Resisting change strikes a fatal blow to an objective self-examination leaving us alone in the dark no longer capable of searching for our true identity and subsequently unable to continue our quest towards discovering the right type of leader.

Critical Point 3

The right type of leader embraces change, whether it is small or large; when ever it is necessary to do so. In fact the right type of leader actively promotes an organizational culture that has an enhanced capacity to learn, adapt, and change.

Critical Point 4

From an organizational perspective, three types of change have been identified: procedural, technological, and systemic.

Critical Point 5

Each of the three types of organizational changes is comprised of six underlying characteristics. Change is: (a) a process, (b) accomplished by individuals, not groups or programs, (c) a highly personal experience, (d) incremental, (e) understand best in terms of one's own practice, and (f) accomplished by focusing upon the individuals involved in the implementation (Zepeda).

Critical Point 6

The bottom line regarding change, whether it is organizational or personal, is that to change means to alter a paradigm.

Critical Point 7

In order for each of us to achieve a higher level of personal growth and maturity we must be willing to make the decision that the paradigms we hold as gospel may need to be changed.

Critical Point 8

The issue now becomes a question of what decision do you want to make? Do you want to take the last step in our journey to discover who you truly are and in the process discover the right type of leader?

Chapter 10

Critical Point 1

The right type of leader can only emerge from an altruistic approach to life.

Critical Point 2

The right type of leader focuses upon the needs of the employees thereby creating a workplace characterized by highly motivated and productive employees who are focused upon satisfying the needs of the customer. In other words, the right type of leader pursues organizational goals and objectives in such a way that the growth and integrity of people are respected. Other characteristics of the right type of leader include: comfortable with people; puts employees first; open-door cheerleader; no reserved parking place, private washroom, or dining room; common touch; good listener; fair; humble; tough, confronts nasty problems; tolerant of disagreement (respectful of the opinion of others); has strong convictions (altruistic approach to life); trusts people; gives credit, takes blame; prefers personal communication over written communication such as memos, email or long reports; keeps promises; and thinks there are at least two other people in the organization who would be good CEOs.

Critical Point 3

CREEPS must always be eliminated from any management or leadership position.

Critical Point 4

The first definitive key to organizational success and sustainability is embodied in the first, three critical points of this chapter.

Chapter 11

Critical Point 1

In most workplaces individuals cannot work alone to satisfy customer needs and accomplish organizational goals. Generally organizational accomplishments are achieved at the group or department level.

Critical Point 2

Groups or departments are impacted by the organizational conditions imposed on the group or department, department member resources, department structure, department processes, and department task.

Critical Point 3

Understanding how to maximize the factors that impact group or department performance constitutes the second definitive key to organizational success and sustainability.

Chapter 12

Critical Point 1

The building blocks of a great to place are like a large, multicolored patchwork quilt consisting of the following concepts: a type "A" organizational culture, putting employees first, the right action principle, social exchange theory, efficiency wages, quality of work life, and career anchors.

Critical Point 2

Only in a great place to work do employees consistently put the forth the maximum work effort.

Critical Point 3

Creating a great place to work is the third definitive key to organizational sustainability and success.

Chapter 13

Critical Point 1

The culture of a nation impacts the chances of organizational success and sustainability.

Critical Point 2

Two models to evaluate the critical attributes of a nation are Porter's Diamond and the International Hough Company Matrix.

Critical Point 3

For organizations that elect to utilize expatriates, the Usable Content Model can serve as a guide for reducing expatriate failure rates.

Critical Point 4

By carefully analyzing the culture with in a nation and providing CCT the chances of obtaining consistent profitability is greatly enhanced; and this realization opens the door to the fourth definitive key of organizational success and sustainability. In short, organizational decision-makers must understand the culture in which their organization operates.

Chapter 14

Critical Point 1

There are four product markets: perfect competition, monopoly, monopolistic competition, and an oligopoly. The number of competitors primarily distinguishes one market from another.

Critical Point 2

An understanding of the strategic planning process will provide a framework for analyzing why an organization exists and how it continues to survive against competing entities.

Critical Point 3

The holy grail of the strategic planning process is to learn how to make better managerial decisions as measured by the competitive advantage that an organization achieves over its rivals.

Critical Point 4

According to Michael Porter an organization can obtain three competitive options: cost leadership, a differentiation strategy, or a focus strategy.

Critical Point 5

Underlying Porter's three competitive strategies are the genetic building blocks of competitive advantage: superior efficiency, superior product quality, superior innovation, and superior customer service or responsiveness.

Organizations that focus on the building blocks of competitive advantage increase the probability of improving the firm's bottom line. Increasing the bottom line is the bottom line!

Critical Point 6

Output value creation stems from the building blocks of competitive advantage.

Critical Point 7

Output value is measured by the equation: $V = B/P$.

Critical Point 8

The skills and abilities of the employees have a critical impact output value.

Critical Point 9

The skills of an employee are determined by the employee's intellectual and physical abilities.

Critical Point 10

Matching an employee's ability to the job increases output value.

Critical Point 11

Ultimately, creating output value is the result of establishing a competitive advantage in the marketplace.

Thus the fifth definitive key to organizational success and sustainability is to achieve a competitive advantage in the marketplace.

Critical Point 12

A chance event can either derail or provide a benefit to an organization and it cannot be planned for, or predicted; chance events just happen.

Critical Point 13

When a chance event occurs, the five definitive keys to organizational success and sustainability have a dramatic influence upon which organizations will thrive and the ones that will become extinct.

Chance events include (but are not limited to) fluctuations in the business cycle, natural disasters, and suddenly changing world events.

Chapter 15

Critical Point 1

It's the five definitive keys that generate maximum output value. Without a true commitment to the five definitive keys at all levels throughout an organization, the journey to enhance organizational performance will be an elusive adventure.

Critical Point 2

The probability of organizational success and sustainability is low when: (a) wrong type of leader; (b) low group (department) productivity; (c) bad place to work; (d) don't understand the culture of the society; and (e) no competitive advantage over competitors.

Critical Point 3

The probability of organizational success and sustainability is high when: (a) right type of leader; (b) high group (department) productivity; (c) great place to work; d) understand the culture of the society; and (e) has a competitive advantage over competitors.

Critical Point 4

A chance event can tilt an outcome in a positive or negative manner for an organization.

Chapter 16

Critical Point 1

The five definitive keys are the principles that govern organizational performance now and in the future and as such summarize organizational performance in a nutshell.

Critical Point 2

Ignore the five definitive keys and jeopardize your organization's ability to achieve organizational success and sustainability.